2004 POET...

ONCE UPON A RHYME

IMAGINATION FOR A NEW GENERATION

Tayside

Edited by Steve Twelvetree

 Young**Writers**

First published in Great Britain in 2005 by:
Young Writers
Remus House
Coltsfoot Drive
Peterborough
PE2 9JX
Telephone: 01733 890066
Website: www.youngwriters.co.uk

SB ISBN 1 84460 646 5

Foreword

Young Writers was established in 1991 and has been passionately devoted to the promotion of reading and writing in children and young adults ever since. The quest continues today. Young Writers remains as committed to engendering the fostering of burgeoning poetic and literary talent as ever.

This year's Young Writers competition has proven as vibrant and dynamic as ever and we are delighted to present a showcase of the best poetry from across the UK. Each poem has been carefully selected from a wealth of *Once Upon A Rhyme* entries before ultimately being published in this, our twelfth primary school poetry series.

Once again, we have been supremely impressed by the overall high quality of the entries we have received. The imagination, energy and creativity which has gone into each young writer's entry made choosing the best poems a challenging and often difficult but ultimately hugely rewarding task - the general high standard of the work submitted amply vindicating this opportunity to bring their poetry to a larger appreciative audience.

We sincerely hope you are pleased with our final selection and that you will enjoy *Once Upon A Rhyme Tayside* for many years to come.

Contents

Jack Harrison (8)   20
Melissa Stephen (9)   20
Lauren Jamieson (8)   21
Amber Renfrey (9)   21
Connor Metcalfe (10)   21

Glenisla Primary School

Serena Archer (9)   22
Adam Forbes (8)   22
Lucy McLean (9)   23
Joss Peters (11)   23
Grace Eadie (7)   24
Jamie Brennan (7)   24
Ailsa Peters (8)   25
Ella Peters (9)   25
Camilla Cumming (10)   26
Fern Peggie (9)   27
Jack Davidson (8)   27

Glenlyon Primary School

Maryanne Helen Drysdale (6)   28
Skye Brettell (7)   28
Meghan Potter (10)   28

Killin Primary School

Megan Rhys (10)   29
Aimee Macleod (10)   29
Lianne Kennedy (11)   30
Billie Graham (11)   30
Hazel Wyllie (11)   31

Kirkmichael Primary School

Alexander Mulholland (9)   32
Danny Finlay (11)   32
Matthew Van Der Veldt (11)   33
Katie Winton (10)   33
Stephanie Curtis (9)   33
Julie Smith (9)   34
Hannah Moore (10)   34
Holly Brown (8)   34

Rebecca Dick (10)   35

Rebecca Dick (10) 35
Emma Poole (10) 35
Tula Mayne (10) 36

Kirkriggs Primary School
Kelly Murray (10) 37
Sophie McInally (9) 37
Kieran Donald (10) 37
Heather Buchanan (9) 38
Hannah Soutar (10) 38
Eilidh Hogg (10) 38
Gregor Smith (10) 39
Gary Cownie (10) 39
Fiona Adam (10) 39
Josh Forbes (10) 40
Blair Geddes (10) 40
Laura Farquhar (9) 40

Luthermuir Primary School
Luke Houghton (11) 41
Steven Ritchie (9) 41
Jo-Anna Bean (11) 41
Kara Carnegie (10) 42
Charlotte McGuile (9) 42
Rashelle Baird (10) 42
Jessica Painter (10) 43
Caroline Park (10) 43
Gavin Simpson (11) 43
Michelle Gibb (10) 44
Shauna McKeogh (10) 44
Emma Slesser (11) 44

Muthill Primary School
Ellen Logan (8) 45
Lorne MacNaughton (8) 45
Leah Riley (8) 46
Karen McCulloch (9) 46
William Roberts (9) 46
Duncan McCallum (8) 47
Rory Stewart (8) 47
Nathan Gannon (8) 47

Rachael Haddow (8)   48
Katy Scott (8)   48
Sarah Rattray   48
Alexander Carpenter (9)   49
Amy Grant (8)   49
Natasha Gill (8)   49
Mae Mackay (7)   50
Claire Gadsby (8)   50
Kieran Allan (9)   50
Katie Murray (8)   51
Corey Boyle   51

Our Lady's Primary School

Semone Butt (9)   51
Aidan Stewart (9)   52
Daniel Buxey (9)   52
Tara Hunter (9)   52
Ciara O'Brien (8)   53
Jade Colvin (8)   53
Katherine Coyle (9)   53
Jordan Moore (10)   54
Anam Qadar (11)   54
Ross Peters (10)   55
Rosie Hanlon (11)   55
Martin Gray (11)   55
Kieran Kane (10)   56
Laura Batchelor (11)   56
Jessica Heymans (11)   56

Straloch Primary School

Katie Purdie (7)   57
Sandy Horne (10)   57
Jessica Purdie (9)   57
Freya Hunter (7)   58
Matthew Michie (7)   58
Alaine Michie (8)   58
Callum Michie (10)   59

The Community School Of Auchterarder

Jonathan Marshall (11)   59
Kayleigh Thom (11)   59

Alan Park (10)	60
Ross Dougan (11)	60
Nicola Docherty (10)	61
Emma MacLaren (11)	61
Robert Main (10)	62
Eilish Syme (9)	62
Siobhan McKillop (9)	62
Cameron Smith (11)	63
Caroline Harrison (11)	63
Samantha Sinclair (11)	64
Kirsty Urquhart (10)	65
Monica Smith (10)	65
Matthew Gordon (11)	66
Lisa Mackie (10)	67
Jordan Cooper (11)	68
Natalie Kerr (10)	68
Sarah Balfour (11)	69
Louise McPhillimy (10)	69
Ryan Simpson (11)	70
Rachel Pirie (10)	70
Liam Smith (11)	71
Kelsey Watson (11)	71
David C Lawrence (10)	72
Eleanor Gibson (11)	72
Kathryn Robertson (10)	73
Charlotte O'Neill (11)	73
Ciaran Anderson (11)	74
Hollie Park (10)	74
Nicolle Moffat (11)	75
Rachel Parr (11)	75
Gemma Mallis (11)	76
Louise Docherty (10)	76
Emma McNamara (9)	77
Kevin Gorlas (11)	77
Ashley Docherty (8)	77
Freya Bachell (10)	78
Amy Ross (11)	78
Lucy C Menzies (10)	79
Hazel Clark (10)	79
Alex Kitch (9)	80
Reon Lewis (9)	80
Jamie Lawrence (8)	80

Alicia Low (8)	81
Eilidh Sinclair (9)	81
Neil Stewart (11)	81
Josh Goold (9)	82
Emily Dewar (9)	82
Georgina Shepherd (9)	82
Kathleen McRostie (9)	83
Heather Forsyth (10)	83
Joshua Watters (10)	83
Amy Wilkie (9)	84
Andrew Langdown (8)	84
Katie Langlands (9)	84
Ruby Cumming (9)	85
Peter Scott (10)	85
Miranda Radley (8)	85
Lisa Welsh (9)	86
Gary Gilmartin (8)	86
Calum Zielinski (9)	86
Marcus Mollison (9)	87
Kieran Smith (8)	87
Kimberley McPhee (9)	87
Lucy O'Neill (8)	88
Mikaela Benett (9)	88
Erin Walker (9)	88
Christie Warren (9)	89
Callum Mackie (8)	89
Jamie-Lee McLean (9)	89
Hamilton Smith (9)	90
Rebecca Anderson (8)	90
Logan Parr (8)	90
Greg Sanders (9)	91
Rebecca Greig (9)	91
Annie Booth (8)	91
Cheryl Marchbank (8)	92
Liam Kirk (9)	92
Katie MacFadyen (10)	92
Richard Saffrey	93
Josh Roy (9)	93
Ewan Burnie (8)	93
Jacqueline Porteous	94
Eliot Short (9)	94
Calum Dann (9)	94

Suzanne Porteous (9)	95
Mhairi Gorlas (8)	95
Alistair Wood (8)	95
Sara Miller (9)	96
Duncan Tait (8)	96
Kimberly Russell (9)	96
Kessiah Pattenden (10)	97

Timmergreens Primary School

Thomas Sinclair (9)	97
Rachel Banks (7)	97
Jill Finlayson (10)	98
Christine McLoughlin (11)	98
Paul Barber (11)	99
Hugh Stewart (11)	99
Conor Howden (9)	100
Katie Esplin (10)	100
Ross Milne (10)	101
Evan A Hill (11)	101
Kris Duff (11)	102
Dayle Fowler (11)	102
Paul Reid (11)	103
Lauren Breach (9)	103
Steven Cadger (11)	104
Luke Shepherd (8)	104
Hannah Kate Cargill (10)	105
Shane Holt (10)	105
Kieran Scott (9)	106
Jamie Goodrum (10)	106
Beth Johnston (11)	107
Niamh Hill (7)	107
Jill Smith (11)	108
Abbie Stewart (11)	108
Lucy Wishart (10)	109
Toni Tindal (9)	109
Alanah Richards (8)	110
Caitlin McLoughlin (9)	110
Kate Richards (9)	111
Zak Kennedy (10)	111
Mia McQuillan (9)	112
Beth Milne (9)	112

The Poems

When It Glowed!

A shining, shimmering, small ball
Rolling across the floor.
Just bigger than a marble,
Swirling mist vanishing into thin air,
Don't stare into it
Or you might be transported through time.
Oh no! Here we go!
We're going into the future!
Where are we?
We are at the time when the dinosaurs
Ruled the sea, Earth and skies.
Oh my! A T-rex!
Run for your life!
Down a hill into a muddy stream
What's this?
Something's glowing in my pocket,
It's that marble!
Let's go into time again.
Hello, what time are we in now?
Look!
There's a unicorn with a sharp horn!
Let's go! Quick!
Before a dragon comes.
Oh good, home at last,
I've still got my marble.
Phew!

Isabelle Hoggmascall (9)
Auchenblae School

The Time Twister

A dark, shimmering fireball
Dropped from the Milky Way planet.
It had sword flaming fireballs shooting out of it.
The time twister was blazing with light
And every colour you can think of
Was blazing with light.
The time twister was spinning so fast
It was starting to make a hole in the road.
It shot straight up into the intergalactic world!
The time twister started to fall,
Then the time twister started to shatter and shatter and shatter,
Then it swirled round,
Smash!
It started to rumble and rumble,
Boom!
The time twister was gone!

Ross Milne (10)
Auchenblae School

The Ball Of Lightning

A ball shone in the middle of the damp, dusty hall
sparks flew out
and started a ring of fire
round the ball.
Tiny, little balls of glitter shot out
and went right through the window
and the sun shone on the ball.
The time twister began to rise
and it went right through the hole in the window.
The time twister rose to the clouds
and bounced off
until it struck a flame of lightning.
It bounced off the cloud
and it hit the time twister.
Then it shattered
iInto a thousand tiny rubies.

Samantha Adams (9)
Auchenblae School

Twisting Through Time

While the time twister flies on,
The small ball sparkles in the middle.
Its fiery colours glisten and shine like stars.
Twisting through time goes the time twister,
Charging through space and time,
Blasting past the Milky Way
Going to its home planet,
Pluto, the ice ball.
Wait!
It's going to collide!
Smash!
Clatter!
The time twister remakes itself in the ice
And there it goes!
Bang!
So that's what hit the Earth.
The time twister explodes.

Luke McCormick (9)
Auchenblae School

Galaxy Collision

A blazing fireball glowing like the sun,
A time twister flying through space like a bullet from a gun.
The time twister speeding through the galaxy,
It's sparking, shining,
The colour is unique.
It's speeding through space
Faster than you can speak.
The time twister is colourful,
It has tiny fire rings.
'Watch out, a spaceman!'
The time twister is whizzing towards him.
Smash!
There it goes,
The spaceman has smashed it!
Microscopic emeralds shoot out
Boom!
It's gone!

Jack Millington (10)
Auchenblae School

The Time Twister

The time twister is a round ball
With lots of colours blasting out of it into the sky.
Golden stars twinkle out of the ball
And start to dance around the room.
Colours of the rainbow shoot round the room
Leaving the ball twirling in the air.
Sparks fly out of it and drop to the ground,
Lightning flashes out of the ball and slides along the roof.
Wind blows round the room
Making the colours go faster and faster.
Thunder shakes the room and the sparks sparkle even more.
Purple and blue paint is splattered on the walls everywhere.
The thunder roars louder
And everything comes to a halt.
Suddenly the ball fades
And all the shining colours follow on.
The whole room is back to normal
Waiting for the time twister to appear again.

Alanah Mills (9)
Auchenblae School

Travelling Through Time

A shining, shimmering, fiery ball,
Swirling around the Milky Way.
Fire shoots from the time twister,
Fire blazes from the time twister.
Whirling mist,
Violet, ruby, gold and silver,
Glowing like a star.
Fiery rings shine inside the time twister,
All the colours of the rainbow
Blazing like the moon,
Travelling forward in time
And travelling backwards in time.
Within the time twister stands a figure
Clothed in gold and red velvet.
His face you cannot see
Only his evil, dark eyes.
Out of the time twister
Lightning shoots everywhere.
The time twister is swirling faster and faster
The time twister is out of control!
The time twister hits a star
And explodes
Into fiery bits of glass!

Lucie Hendry (9)
Auchenblae School

A Box Of Secrets

(Inspired by 'Magic Box' by Kit Wright)

In a box of secrets I would put . . .
An elf that never died,
A small whale,
The sound of a sign complaining of sore feet.

In a box of secrets I would put . . .
The taste of my granny's home-made jam,
The feel of baby skin after just being washed,
A cold sun.

In a box of secrets I would put . . .
A squared planet,
The smell of cake slowing rising in the oven,
Hot icicles slowing freezing.

In a box of secrets I would put . . .
Bagpipes being played by a mouse,
The sound of rock falling off the top of the Grand Canyon,
Peppers pulled out of the ground.

Calum Thomson (10)
Barnhill Primary School

My Amazing Magical Box

(Inspired by 'Magic Box' by Kit Wright)

I shall find in my box . . .
The flames of a dragon as it flies through the air.
The shout of two armies as they meet in battle.

I shall find in my box . . .
The smell of a sauna, warm and comforting.
The smooth feel of water as you step in the pool.
Sharks swimming in the sea.

I shall find in my box . . .
A human alien and a soft rock.
A dumb genius and a slow bee
And an ant who did not like company.

Robbie Griffin (11)
Barnhill Primary School

My Magic Box

(Inspired by 'Magic Box' by Kit Wright)

I will put in my box . . .
The smell of a rose starting to open,
A soft snowman standing beside a small swallow,
A red-hot blaze of burning sun.

I will put in my box . . .
The sound of a star twinkling in the pitch-black sky,
A purple and blue sun,
The feel of an icicle melting in your warm hands.

I will put in my box . . .
The taste of chocolate melting on your pink tongue,
A piece of sand that's scared to swim,
The *sssssss* of a snake stirring across the soil.

Hayley Irvine (10)
Barnhill Primary School

My Fantastic Box

(Inspired by 'Magic Box' by Kit Wright)

I will put in my box . . .
A blast of fire from the pit of the core,
The monster's roar from a ferocious lion,
The smell of cake being baked.

I will put in my box . .
Adam's magic golden pendant,
A slow speed boat,
I will put in a giant mouse.

I will put in my box . . .
A fast snail,
The feel of a newborn kitten,
A pillar from under the Tay Bridge
Complaining about standing all the time.

Aaron Selbie (10)
Barnhill Primary School

The Amazing Ball - The Earth
(Inspired by 'Magic box' by Kit Wright)

I will look in the ball . . .
At the loud toot of a small flute,
And the break of day burning backwards,
The smell of a sweet sandy beach.

I will look in the ball . . .
At the chilling breeze from a winter sun,
And the burning wind from a hot blizzard,
The feel of delicious hot chocolate before bed.

I will look in the ball . . .
At the small tortoise who lost his helmet,
And the person who abseiled down a small stone.

I would call my ball, Earth.

Stuart McCarthy (10)
Barnhill Primary School

My Secretive Box
(Inspired by 'Magic Box' by Kit Wright)

I will put in my box . . .
A coloured rainbow that is beautiful and bright.
The whistle of the wind blowing the leaves.
The smell of freshly cut grass.

I will put in my box . . .
The taste of chocolate touching your lips.
A screeching scream from somebody special.
A super-fast snail who raced a car.

I will put in my box . . .
Seven tall dwarves lazy at work.
The whine of a whale who's allergic to water.
The very first sparkle from the very first star.

Rachel Hutton (10)
Barnhill Primary School

My Extraordinary Box

(Inspired by 'Magic Box' by Kit Wright)

I will add to my box . . .
A god's flying elephant covered in a sparkling gold colour,
A song from a genie's golden guitar,
The smell of a cake just out the oven (and baked by a king).

I will add to my box . . .
The feel of a newborn cat,
The taste of melting chocolate made by a dragon,
A baby lion lying by a lucky lake.

I will add to my box . . .
A cold fire in a huge cottage,
A black star sitting on a seat,
A flying tree eating all the birds.

I will add to my box . . .
The call of a crocodile crawling through a crystal castle,
A meteor stuck in a dry sea,
A pirate on a flying spaceship on the great Mars Sea.

These are the things that make my box extraordinary.

Nicholas Forbes (10)
Barnhill Primary School

My Magic Box

(Inspired by 'Magic Box' by Kit Wright)

I will put in my box . . .
The warm golden sunshine on a hot summer's day.
The windy breeze of one autumn's day.
The lovely smell of honeysuckle climbing up the wall.

I will put in my box . . .
The taste of warm pancakes sprinkled with sugar.
The silver sparkle of that shooting star.
The pearlish gleam of the moon at night.

Francesca Allanson (10)
Barnhill Primary School

My Fantasy Box

(Inspired by 'Magic Box' by Kit Wright)

I will put in my box . . .
A glittering, gleaming, glaring sword still stuck in the stone,
The buzzing of an electric eel swimming swiftly in the sea,
A barking cat and a squeaking dog.

I will put in my box . . .
Frightening fire from a phoenix,
A dazzling dagger digging deeply in the box,
The smell of sweet strawberries swaying in the breeze.

I will put in my box . . .
A plane sounding like a tree complaining of stiffness,
A giant squirrel swimming in a small, dry puddle,
A balloon complaining of feeling a bit airy.

Daniel Tait (10)
Barnhill Primary School

My Secret Box

(Inspired by 'Magic Box' by Kit Wright)

I will put in my secret box . . .
The rushing rabbit in Wonderland,
The *sh sh* of the waves beating against the rocks,
The smell of a baking cake in the oven.

I will put in my secret box . . .
The touch of soft fur gliding through my hand,
The taste of rhubarb going down your throat,
A snake snaking its way through sacks of sesame seeds.

I will put in my secret box . . .
The clock of Big Ben with sore hands,
An owl that is afraid of the dark,
An active tortoise that ran in the Olympics.

Mark Pandrich (9)
Barnhill Primary School

My Fantastic Box

(Inspired by 'Magic Box' by Kit Wright)

I will put into my box . . .
A flying carpet whooshing in the wind.
The soft, silky fur of a rabbit.
A boiling snowman on lava in Wales.
A caring, loving killer.

I will put into my box . . .
The exhilarating smell of Galaxy chocolate.
A tiny blue whale in a puddle.
The scent of lavender massage oils.
The very bottom brick of the Eiffel Tower with backache.

Callum Fernie (9)
Barnhill Primary School

My Extraordinary Shoe Box

(Inspired by 'Magic Box' by Kit Wright)

I will put in my box . . .
A magic crystal that Merlin the wizard had on his staff.
The taste of tangy tangerines twisting my tongue.
An eighth day of the week.

I will put in my box . . .
The wind being swished over an Indian night.
Ella's everlasting egg plantation erupting on the Empire's palace.
A square wheel on a car.

I will put in my box . . .
The smell of a baby being showered in talcum powder.
A fast turtle complaining about being fast.
Rising rabbit rampaging through a running river.

David Morton (10)
Barnhill Primary School

My Unusual Trinket Box

(Inspired by 'Magic Box' by Kit Wright)

I will put in my trinket box . . .
A unicorn's horn sprinkled in fairy dust.
A wordless dictionary.
The sound of church bells in the morning.

I will put in my trinket box . . .
The fresh new feel of my mum's bed.
Little Red Riding Hood's blue cloak.
The first horse put on the carousel that gets dizzy easily.

I will put in my trinket box . . .
The taste of fluffy cotton-like candyfloss.
The smell of fish and chips with salt and vinegar.
The crispy crunching sound of snow.

That's what I will put in my trinket box.

Caitlin McKay (10)
Barnhill Primary School

My Secret Box

(Inspired by 'Magic Box' by Kit Wright)

I will put in my box . . .
A shining hair from the head of a beautiful princess.
A soft, silky swish of silk in summer
And a vegetarian tiger.

I will put in my box . . .
A dog taking an owner for a walk.
A mouse hunting an owl and a camel in Antarctica.

I will put in my box . . .
The amazement of an eclipse.
The magic of something being born.
The eerie cry of a dying star.

Catherine Waller (9)
Barnhill Primary School

My Extraordinary Box

(Inspired by 'Magic Box' by Kit Wright)

I will put in my box . . .
The dancing dragon of China,
The smell of the grass after being sprayed,
The rubber that doesn't rub out.

I will put in my box . . .
The shark that had no teeth,
The tiny blue whale,
The 10ft baby.

I will put in my box . . .
The burning ice cream,
The dolphin that can't jump,
The Leaning Tower of Pisa's top brick is very, very dizzy.

Scott Fraser (9)
Barnhill Primary School

My Fantasy Box

(Inspired by 'Magic Box' by Kit Wright)

I will put in my box . . .
A sun with no light,
The howl of a fancy, frosty wind,
The smell of crusty brown bread rising in an oven.

I will put in my box . . .
The feel of a nice clean dog,
The first bubble from a champagne bottle,
The taste of twisty, turning toothpaste.

I will put in my box . . .
A blue sparrow singing quietly with a giant voice,
The dry sea getting as wet as possible,
The taste of brilliant brown chocolate melting over my tongue.

Callum Lyall (10)
Barnhill Primary School

My Fantasy Box

(Inspired by 'Magic Box' by Kit Wright)

I shall put in my box . . .
The ripeness of juicy fruit.
The sound of the wind whistling my favourite song in a summer breeze.
The smell of sweet, milky chocolate melting in the sun.

I shall put in my box . . .
The sight of a swallow soaring into the safe sky.
The driest raindrop touching the wettest fire.
The only glue without a stick.

I shall put in my box . . .
The taste of apple pie with sweet sugar and deep crust.
The homesick girl crying in her home.
The happiness of a giant smile.

I shall put in my box . . .
The tickle of my dog sniffing my skin.
Friendly flowers floating in faraway forests.
The largest ocean in the smallest sea.

Beth Ritchie (10)
Barnhill Primary School

My Secret Box

(Inspired by 'Magic Box' by Kit Wright)

I will put in my box . . .
The hottest snowman I know,
The black thunder which came from the yellow phoenix,
The coldest star and the hottest moon.

I will put in my box . . .
The blackest sea that I have ever swam in,
The first smile from the oldest baby,
The smell of the whitest fire I have ever smelt.

Ross Suttie (9)
Barnhill Primary School

My Magic Box

(Inspired by 'Magic Box' by Kit Wright)

I will put in my box . . .
The shimmering light of the daylight sun,
A laugh that is heard miles and miles away,
The smell of babies when they are out of the bath.

I will put in my box . . .
A feel of a rabbit touching your skin,
The taste of sweets melting in your mouth,
The tip of the Statue of Liberty afraid of heights.

I will put in my box . . .
A silent song from a small snake,
The song of a dolphin who can't sing,
A friendly guard dog lazing about.

I will put in my box . . .
A jellyfish that can walk over the sea,
A snowman built on an autumn day,
And a song from a baby bird falling from the sky.

Ashleigh Grant (10)
Barnhill Primary School

My Magic Box

(Inspired by 'Magic Box' by Kit Wright)

A beautiful, shiny bike with flashing lights,
The smell of burgers in the sky.

I will put in my box . . .
The flash of fireworks, the bang of a firework.

I will put in my box . . .
Some of the water from every sea in the world,
And the taste of bananas and strawberries.

Blair Cochrane (9)
Barnhill Primary School

My Secret Box

(Inspired by 'Magic Box' by Kit Wright)

I will put in my secret box . . .
A sparkling gold teddy bear,
The smell of a newly grown rose,
The feel of the hot-water bottle touching.

I will put in my secret box . . .
Leafy Liam's loud laugh,
The barking of a cat
And the sound of a midnight wave from the warm sea.

I will put in my secret box . . .
The taste of a newly caught golden fish,
The ice hanging on a hot day
And silly Simon's secret sausage.

Elliot Hunter (10)
Barnhill Primary School

My Cool Box

(Inspired by 'Magic Box' by Kit Wright)

I will put in my box . . .
A magic fairy from a film,
A shimmering snake slithering slowly,
The sea moving very slowly.

I will put in my box . . .
The taste of terrific toffee,
The sound of super sweets singing,
A dictionary with just pictures.

Erin Johnson (9)
Barnhill Primary School

Love

Love is pink like a colourful bunch of flowers,
It sounds like water trickling,
It tastes like vanilla ice cream,
It looks like a cosy bed,
It feels like my pony's fur against my face,
It smells like a bright red rose,
It reminds me of a picture full of ponies with hearts on them.

Becky Macdonald (10)
Glenbervie Primary School

Happiness

Happiness is yellow like the shining sand on the beach,
It sounds like the laughter of cheerful children,
It tastes like melting ice cream on your tongue,
It looks like people playing in the playground,
It feels like I'm flying in the sky on my pony at night passing the moon,
It smells like flowers in a vase beside me,
It reminds me of my pony galloping around the field.

Kirsty Alexander (10)
Glenbervie Primary School

Happiness

Happiness is yellow like the scorching sun
It sounds like birds singing on a wonderful bright summer's morning.
It tastes like Mackies butterscotch ice cream.
It looks like a combine slowly chugging away
through the golden fields of corn.
It feels like flying through the air in a hot air balloon.
It smells like lots of lovely flowers in a vase.
It reminds me of summer and all the lovely flowers
when harvest is underway.

Alistair McBain (10)
Glenbervie Primary School

Love

Love is pink like roses swaying in the breeze,
It sounds like birds singing in a choir,
It tastes like biting into a juicy red apple,
It looks like a litter of cute kittens,
It feels like a beautiful sunflower,
It smells like a field of lovely daffodils,
It reminds me of a dog jumping up and licking my face.

Hayley Reid (9)
Glenbervie Primary School

Silence

Silence is white like snow drifting in the breeze,
It sounds like a breeze swooshing through the trees,
It tastes like white rice from China,
It looks like an empty room painted white and filled with lightness,
It feels like an empty echoing cave,
It smells like mushrooms growing in a muddy field,
It reminds me of my sister's tonsillitis.

Jack Harrison (8)
Glenbervie Primary School

Anger

Anger is red like flames in the fire,
It sounds like a raging lion,
It tastes like a maggot with mould all over,
It looks like a fighting army with guns,
It feels like when you cut your knee,
It smells like horrid chemicals with poison,
It reminds me of a cyclone ripping through the town!

Melissa Stephen (9)
Glenbervie Primary School

Love

Love is red like a basket of roses,
It sounds like the lips of somebody kissing someone on the cheek,
It tastes like a jar of strawberry jam,
It looks like a bed of roses in my garden,
It feels like a blanket of fluff on top of me,
It smells like a bowl of strawberries with a blanket of sugar on top,
It reminds me of all my friends playing with me at playtime.

Lauren Jamieson (8)
Glenbervie Primary School

Anger

Anger is red like an explosion of fire,
It sounds like a lion roaring in a cage of lava,
It tastes like a red-hot chilli on my insides,
It looks like a boulder about to fall on me,
It feels like death about to strike,
It smells like cold blood dripping from a cut,
It reminds me of a fiery dragon in the night sky.

Amber Renfrey (9)
Glenbervie Primary School

Fear

Fear is white like an empty room,
It sounds like a person screaming,
It tastes like a sour lemon lollipop,
It looks like a shocked face,
It feels like a shaking bird crying,
It smells like a rotten body,
It reminds me of my heart thumping.

Connor Metcalfe (10)
Glenbervie Primary School

Northumbrians Attack

A man comes running
Warriors approaching, he screams
People panic
Children hide
Slapping woad on our faces
We grab our heavy swords

We hurdle onto our horses
And race down the hill
At the bottom, I see the enemy
Swords held high, glistening in the sun

We meet with a deafening roar
Ear-piercing screams
Clashing blades
Arrows thudding into bodies
Pools of red gathering on the ground

The noise starts to die down
Looking around
Northumbrians lie on the ground
We are victorious.

Serena Archer (9)
Glenisla Primary School

Battle Of Dunnichen

The clatter of swords and the cry of pain.
The sound of spears bouncing off the metal shields.
The twang of the bow as arrows shoot through the air.
Some reach their target.
I see blood trickle down.

Adam Forbes (8)
Glenisla Primary School

Battle Of Dunnichen

A huntsman announces the enemy's arrival
Every Pict emerges from his thatch roofed home
Farmers, craftsmen, builders,
Spinners, weavers, cooks,
Now become warriors,
Decorating their mud splattered faces
With blue Celtic designs.
They grab spears, swords, shields and arrows
Crafted by their own rough-skinned hands.
The tension is mounting.
Running down the hill, hiding behind boulders,
Hearing the galloping hooves, preparing to fight,
Arrows soar, swords clash, spears pierce metal shields.
Unlucky warriors fall heavily to the ground.
Sounds of battle fade.
King Bridei defeats King Egfrith of Northumbria.

Lucy McLean (9)
Glenisla Primary School

Battle Of Dunnichen

The silence was broken by a sea of violence
I roared in anger at these invaders!
As I stabbed with my shrapnel spear
I could hear the screams of wounded and dying warriors.

The blue dye on my face gave me strength
even though it seemed to be splattered
with the unmistakable red of blood.

I brought darkness down on Northumbrian eyes
as I felt my deadly sword pierce more flesh
I did not like killing.
There was no joy in violence
but I must show them no mercy and fight
for the freedom which we deserve.
The Picts must not be defeated.

Joss Peters (11)
Glenisla Primary School

Fighting At The Battle Of Dunnichen

A messenger comes,
'Horsemen approaching,
We'll be attacked!'

I painted my face
With the blue woad dye.
I felt braver now.

Grabbing my sword
I ran from my home of wattle and daub
Down the hill, terrified, shaking,
My heart beating faster by the minute.

Splashing through the watery ditch
I hold my sword in the air
The battle begins!

I say to myself,
'We must win the battle
King Egfrith must die.'
The Northumbrians must leave the Picts alone.

Grace Eadie (7)
Glenisla Primary School

Battle Of Nechtansmere

Steam rises from the metal cooking pot.
A woman spins some wool.
Another weaves it into a cloak.

A man came running.
He raged, *'Horsemen arriving!'*

We did not like when the battle began.
We got our weapons and ran.
We got our horses and charged.
Some of us were injured, some of us died.

Jamie Brennan (7)
Glenisla Primary School

Dunnichen

A messenger cries out,
'An army approaching!'

Fear made my heart hammer against my chest.
Grabbing my weapons I mount my horse.
Charging down from the hill fort on top of Dunnichen.

I raise my sword as the battle begins.

I hear roars of warriors, screams of pain
I smell sweaty bodies, I sense the fear
I see blood dripping from wounded bodies.

We Picts must fight as long as it takes
Bridei our king leads us forward
Till the last of Egfrith's army is dead!

Ailsa Peters (8)
Glenisla Primary School

Northumbrian Attack

Northumbrians approach
Panic strikes the hill fort!
Pictish warriors prepare for battle,
Decorating their faces
With blue woad and Celtic designs
To intimidate the enemy.
Gathering their weapons for battle
They charge down from Dunnichen Hill
Drawing their swords, raising their spears and shaking with fear.

The battle begins!
Swords clash and splinter against metal shields
Yells and screams of pain resound from wounded warriors.
Finally the Picts win the fight.
The proud King Bridei leads the last of his warriors
Back to their hill fort home.

Ella Peters (9)
Glenisla Primary School

Battle Of Nechtansmere

The sun was rising.
A messenger came running.
Horsemen were approaching.
The peaceful and quiet hill fort
Became noisy as the panic spread.

Grabbing my sword
And decorating my face in woad.
I ran down the hill
Along with the rest of the Pictish army.

Splashing through the ditch
And brandishing my sword
Its blade flashing in the sun
I think to myself
We must win battle
We must defeat the Northumbrians.

We meet halfway down the hill
Swords clashing
Shields splintered
Spears pierced
Men fall heavily to the ground.

I swing my sword defensively
Killing anyone who comes in my reach
The battle sounds fade away
The Picts were victorious.

King Bridei leads the rest of his army
Back to the hill fort.

Camilla Cumming (10)
Glenisla Primary School

Prepare To Fight

Horsemen approaching.
We must prepare to fight.
I grab my sword and swipe the blade.
Sunlight catches the steel.
Smearing woad on my face.
We run down the hill shouting.

My heart is racing.
I feel scared and nervous.
No time to turn back.

My sword piercing.
Arrows flying overhead.
Injured men screaming.
Fighting men roaring.
I am terrified.

The roaring starts to die.
The fighting is all over.
We have won.

Fern Peggie (9)
Glenisla Primary School

Battle Of Dunnichen

Swords clashing
Men yelling
Dying
As the battle goes on
Blood everywhere.
Blue faced warriors charging down from the hill fort
Fighting for their country.
Northumbrians lying dead on the ground
Wounded Picts covered in blood.

Jack Davidson (8)
Glenisla Primary School

Untitled

A warm, furry coat, sharp teeth like a pencil
The tiger is sleeping under the trees
He roars like an elephant
He smells an antelope
He hears an elephant
A hunter tries to catch him
The tiger tastes the meat.

Maryanne Helen Drysdale (6)
Glenlyon Primary School

Untitled

Silky coat, sharp teeth like knives
Glittering in the moon, purring loudly
He smells something like an antelope
He hears something trotting
A hunter sees the tiger
The tiger tastes the antelope.

Skye Brettell (7)
Glenlyon Primary School

The Tiger

His coat is soft, smooth and stripy
Sharp teeth like shiny knives gleaming in the dark
Creeping in the dark jungle quietly
He roars like a raging tornado
He smells the blood of an antelope
He hears the screeching of the monkey
He creeps through the jungle like a hunter
He finds his prey and rips it apart.

Meghan Potter (10)
Glenlyon Primary School

That's Disgusting

There was a young boy called Jack,
Who went to put on his mac,
But on the inside
His sister put pies,
And the pies were all crusty and black.

There was a young girl called Jess
Who made such a terrible mess,
And to her disgust
She found that she must
Wear a luminous yellow dress.

Megan Rhys (10)
Killin Primary School

The Crazy Cat

There was a very crazy cat,
Whose name was Postman Pat,
He was black and white,
But not very bright,
He liked to sit on your lap.

The postman's name was Jess,
Whose hair was always a mess,
If the post was late,
He got in a state
He liked to wear a dress.

Aimee Macleod (10)
Killin Primary School

The Funny Family

Mum, Dad and kids,
All as daft as twits,
Lived in a house
And had a pet mouse
And lived with Granny who knits.

There was daft Dad,
Who was really mad,
He was football crazy,
And also very lazy,
Daft Dad was never sad.

Then there was mad Mum,
Who was really dumb,
She did her tables,
In the stables,
She even sucked her thumb.

Then there was Sister Suzie,
Who liked to eat museli,
She was never clean,
And always mean,
Sister Suzie was very spooky.

Last was little Bill,
Who sat on the window sill,
He thought it was funny,
When he sucked his dummy
And he liked to climb up the hill.

Lianne Kennedy (11)
Killin Primary School

Billie

There once was a boy called Billie
Who was incredibly silly
So when he pulled down his pants
And let in some ants
He wriggled on home, poor Billie.

Billie Graham (11)
Killin Primary School

The Freaky Family

The freaky family live in space,
And always eat posh chairs,
People think they're aliens,
Even the big mayor!

The freaky family's dad,
Is very, very mad,
He dances around like a dog,
And loves to kiss a hog,
That's the family's dad!

The freaky family's mum,
Loves to hit her bum,
Her face has turned blue,
Because she doesn't wear any shoes,
That's the family's mum!

The freaky family's daughter
Could weirdly live underwater,
Her hair felt like glue
And her favourite word was, 'Moo!'
That's the family's daughter.

The freaky family's son,
Loved to play in the sun,
His skin went all tanned,
Like the colour of ploughed land,
That's the family's son!

The freaky family live in space,
And always wear pretty lace,
They sleep on chairs,
With loads of bears,
That's the freaky family!

Hazel Wyllie (11)
Killin Primary School

Maurice

Maurice he slinks through the shadows,
Then as quick as a louse,
He leaps upon an unsuspecting mouse!
He yowls in triumph!
The kill is done!
Then he pads into a bush,
And eats his mouse quietly.
Amber eyes glowing,
He pads across the gravel,
And *miaow!*
An extremely fat cat,
Walks into the courtyard . . .
Slash! The cat slashes Maurice,
Slash! Maurice slashes the cat.
Reeeooowww! The cat,
Pads away.
Maurice now has a claw,
In his ear.
He hisses at the cat,
Then slinks away.

Alexander Mulholland (9)
Kirkmichael Primary School

Weather

Lightning, lightning it's so frightening.
Thunder, thunder it likes to wonder.
Rain, rain it's a pain.
Snow, snow it's aglow.
Sun, sun it's so fun.
Hail, hail it's a gale.

Danny Finlay (11)
Kirkmichael Primary School

Space Is Big

Space, space is a wonderful place.
Lots of stars,
Lots of planets,
Things to see and things to touch.
The universe is a very big place,
Black holes are dangerous,
And space is a very, very big place.

Matthew Van Der Veldt (11)
Kirkmichael Primary School

Adventure

Come on everybody,
Get up now,
We're going on an adventure,
Oh wow,
Nobody's not coming,
Everyone's here,
We might even spot a couple of deer,
And when we come home we shall be tired
From our adventure.
But we admired it
And we shall put our heads on our pillows and sleep.

Katie Winton (10)
Kirkmichael Primary School

A Poem That's Very Short

I know this poem isn't very long,
But if I had a choice
I'd turn it into a song.
I told you this wasn't very long,
So you should have listened,
And not have read on.

Stephanie Curtis (9)
Kirkmichael Primary School

The Old Castle Door

People wonder what lurks,
Behind the old widow castle door.
Is it a monster?
Or is it mice scattering around the floor.
Going squeak, squeak.
But then one day someone opened the door.
And then, *'Boo!'*
Then the person was never seen again.
But what was it?

Julie Smith (9)
Kirkmichael Primary School

Thunder And Lightning

Lightning, lightning everywhere,
It sometimes gives me quite a scare,
Lightning, lightning you're so frightening,
Lightning, lightning you're so blinding,
Lightning, lightning with your flash,
You sometimes give me quite a rash.

Thunder, thunder it's a blunder,
Thunder, thunder I do wonder,
Thunder, thunder makes a noise,
It frightens all the girls and boys.

Hannah Moore (10)
Kirkmichael Primary School

Love Is Nice

Love is sweet as a dove
Love is so sweet like the moon
Love is so gentle like stars
But sometimes love can do bad things
But don't worry, because fairies can help.

Holly Brown (8)
Kirkmichael Primary School

Weather

Thunder, thunder how I wonder
How scary you are
Rush up to your bed
When you hear me bang.
Lightning, lightning how scary you are
When you flash your yellow flash
You give me quite a dash
And I rush up to my bed.
Sun, sun you're such great fun
When you're out you make me go in or burn.
Snow, snow you are so cold
You make me go inside.
Clouds, clouds you're so grey
You bring me the rain every day.
Rain, rain you bring so much
You sometimes flood the place.
Hail, hail is the best
You make me laugh.

Rebecca Dick (10)
Kirkmichael Primary School

Everything

The sun shines as the sky goes by.
The Earth moves as the flowers bloom.
The snow is white as a kite is bright.
People walk down the street as they meet.
A car drives as a plane flies.
Stars rise as they drive.
Coming outside as the noise rises.
Wolves howl as cats go miaow
And sleeping at night is a fright.

Emma Poole (10)
Kirkmichael Primary School

My Class

Katie is so clever and also very nice,
I like her very much and she likes me,
She is almost always happy except at exams,
But I really like it when her and I are mad!

Rebecca is so nice and also very clever,
I like her and she likes me,
I really, really like her when she is very happy,
But I get really upset when she is sad!

Hannah is so pretty with her reddish hair and brown eyes,
I like her and she likes me,
Sometimes we are not friends,
Then I feel quite sad!

Anna is so nice and also very bright,
I like her and she likes me,
She is almost always happy except when she gets the blame,
Then I feel quite sad!

Heather is so nice with her fair blonde hair,
I like her and she likes me,
She looks so very pretty with the sun on her hair,
But I really like her when she has a nice big smile!

Emma is so nice with her sparkling blue eyes,
I like her and she likes me,
She is very good at maths and lots of other stuff,
But I really like her when she is being silly!

Julie is so clever and also very nice,
I like her and she likes me,
She looks very pretty with hair and eyes,
But I really like it when her and I are friends!

So you see I like all my class,
But I really like it when they are loopy mad!

Tula Mayne (10)
Kirkmichael Primary School

Detention

From the window I can see
The sun shining down on me
Like a ball of golden wool
It's a pity I am in school.

From the window I can see
A place where I want to be,
Children running and having fun
I'll have to get my sums done.

Kelly Murray (10)
Kirkriggs Primary School

My World

Earth is round, blue and green
Far away yet it can be seen
Some countries are hot, some are cold
It swirls around all day long,
Like it's dancing and saying,
'You can join in.'
It is surrounded by planets, stars and the sun,
And you always know when the day is done
Cos the moon will come out then night has begun.

Sophie McInally (9)
Kirkriggs Primary School

Kennings Penalty Shoot Out

Short-hitter
Goal-kicker
Penalty-stopper
Goal-whopper
Bad-tackler!
Good-battler
Goal-striker
What a fighter!

Kieran Donald (10)
Kirkriggs Primary School

Camping Through The Summer

Along the winding, bumpy road
Along the twisting, curvy road
Along the straight road to the caravan park,
Hooray!

Staying in a tiny little caravan packed with furniture
Two bunk beds and a double bed,
Camping under the night sky,
Watching the world go by.

Heather Buchanan (9)
Kirkriggs Primary School

Red Devil

A big fire-breathing bull
Chilli ball bursting into flames
A huge bowl of tomato soup
A tree trunk filled with hot peppers
A sticky bubble bath,
The volcano is angry.

Hannah Soutar (10)
Kirkriggs Primary School

Maths

Times tables,
just about able,
subtraction sums,
I twiddle my thumbs.
The answers spin
around in my head,
*I want to do
art instead!*

Eilidh Hogg (10)
Kirkriggs Primary School

Nessie

All green and very scaly.
Like a huge railway
All fat and puffed.
He looks very tough.
He swims about looking proud.
'What a big thing!' I shout out aloud.

Gregor Smith (10)
Kirkriggs Primary School

Little Snowflake

I was asleep when I saw a snowflake,
The coldness of the snow made me wake.
All the snowflakes seemed really quite small
It's the ice on the ground that makes them fall.

A snowflake itself is a bit of a shiver
If one falls down your back it makes you quiver!
Snowflakes melt if they hit the path,
One landed on my head and made me laugh.

Snowflakes make a lovely scene
Almost like a surreal dream.

Gary Cownie (10)
Kirkriggs Primary School

From My Window

From my window what do I see?
Birds singing in a tree
Bees are humming all around
Summer sun is fading now
The farmer gets the plough
Animals gathering food
Soon we'll be in a festival mood.

Fiona Adam (10)
Kirkriggs Primary School

From My Window . . .

Sun shining in the sky
Children playing with their balls,
An artist drawing a small picture,
I can also see a dog playing with its stick,
It is beautiful today,
It is a lovely sunny day, again.

Josh Forbes (10)
Kirkriggs Primary School

My Pet

A little furball
With ears that hang down,
Small and fluffy and full of fun,
It likes to eat any food like carrots and cabbage.

It likes to cuddle into you and lick your finger,
It has two big front teeth that hang over its bottom lip
My rabbit is cute and cuddly,
Just like me!

Blair Geddes (10)
Kirkriggs Primary School

Earth

The Earth is like a green and blue ball
Something you kick into a goal.

It turns so slowly, very slowly
Like a balloon that's stuck in a hole.

It's going to drift to another planet
Far, far away.

It's going to sail on an ocean bed
One rainy day.

Laura Farquhar (9)
Kirkriggs Primary School

Darkness

Darkness is as dark as the midnight sky
It looks like a big black spot
It feels like the thin air
It reminds me of a bad day
Darkness sounds like a silent room
It tastes like the cold air
It smells like the cold, plain air
Around us every day.

Luke Houghton (11)
Luthermuir Primary School

Darkness

Darkness is black like the night sky
It smells like sour milk
It feels like getting a punch in the face
It tastes evil and foul
It sounds like low piano notes
Darkness reminds me of Hallowe'en
Darkness looks like a blanket with nothing else on it.

Steven Ritchie (9)
Luthermuir Primary School

Darkness

Darkness is black like a hollow skull,
It looks like a wolf's shining red eyes,
Darkness feels like a sinister secret,
It tastes like evil rotting skin,
Darkness smells like blood in a river,
Darkness sounds like a werewolf in the woods,
Darkness reminds me of Lord Voldemort.

Jo-Anna Bean (11)
Luthermuir Primary School

Darkness

Darkness is black like midnight
Darkness reminds me of wolves when they howl
Darkness tastes cold and scary and makes you feel bad
Darkness smells like mould and makes you feel sick
Darkness sounds quiet and cold
Darkness feels really scary and frightening
Darkness looks like black clouds.

Kara Carnegie (10)
Luthermuir Primary School

Happiness

Happiness is white like a gleaming star,
Happiness makes you feel warm and relaxed,
Happiness sounds like the cool breeze blowing through my hair,
Happiness looks like a night full of stars,
Happiness reminds me of a big fancy wedding,
Happiness smells like a big chocolate bar,
Happiness tastes like chocolate ice cream,
Happiness is a good life that you would want to have!

Charlotte McGuile (9)
Luthermuir Primary School

Happiness

Happiness is white like a shooting star.
It looks like a row of stars singing and leaping.
It feels like a beautiful dream.
It tastes foul and air fills your mouth with clear wind.
Happiness smells of clear breeze.
Happiness reminds me of when my aunt was alive.
Happiness is blowing in my ears.

Rashelle Baird (10)
Luthermuir Primary School

Darkness

Darkness is black like the night sky
It feels like evil is all around
Darkness smells like a dead person has come alive
It tastes like you have rotten skin in your mouth
Darkness sounds like someone being tortured
It looks like a snake's red eyes
Darkness reminds me of Lord Voldemort!

Jessica Painter (10)
Luthermuir Primary School

Happiness

Happiness is yellow and is like a sunflower.
Happiness looks like a big smiley sunshine.
Happiness smells like strawberries.
Happiness tastes like a chocolate chip cake.
Happiness reminds me of happy memories.
Happiness sounds like people laughing.

Caroline Park (10)
Luthermuir Primary School

Darkness

Darkness is black like a dark cat with stormy yellow eyes
Darkness reminds me of Most Haunted
Darkness feels dizzy and I have nowhere to go
Darkness looks like nothing or a big black dot
Darkness smells strongly of burning bushes
Darkness tastes like cold breezy air
Darkness sounds like feet crunching all around me.

Gavin Simpson (11)
Luthermuir Primary School

Darkness

Darkness is black like an eerie shadow,
Darkness smells rancid and disgusting,
It reminds me of being a prisoner in my own room,
It sounds like witches and monsters shouting
                                and screaming in my ears,
It tastes like revolting, stale milk,
Darkness looks like an enormous, dark black hole,
Darkness makes you feel terrified.

Michelle Gibb (10)
Luthermuir Primary School

Darkness

Darkness is black like the silent night,
It reminds me of a squawking blackbird,
It smells like melted chocolate!
It feels like a big hollow pit,
It tastes like dust in my mouth,
It sounds so silent
All I can hear is the river flowing by,
It looks like a big, black panther ready to pounce.

Shauna McKeogh (10)
Luthermuir Primary School

Frost

Frost is clear like a transparent glass window.
Frost looks like crystals shimmering on the lawn.
Frost feels chilly and damp and makes me shiver.
Frost tastes like really stale water in a cup.
Frost smells really frosty and cold and dewy.
Frost reminds me of snow and Christmas.
Frost tingles my fingers and makes me cold.

Emma Slesser (11)
Luthermuir Primary School

Voice Of Doom

V ultures swoop black as night
O ily and wet sucking you up
I cily sizzling like a smokey fire
C autiously you step forward
E ventually it's swirling towards you

O ver trees, over bushes,
F ighting to reach you.

D evouring plants, crops
O ther things don't stand a chance
O ncoming, never stopping
M any flee before it . . .
It is the voice of doom!

Ellen Logan (8)
Muthill Primary School

Crystal Snow

As the snow gently hits the ground.
I feel very light, almost like a feather.
Of course I don't mind the weather.
It looks like . . . creamy fog.
Yet it's as still as a sleeping dog.
It also sounds like pattering feet
Longing to get to a seat.
It smells wonderfully of
Ice cream in a cone
Well . . .
It's not unknown.

Lorne MacNaughton (8)
Muthill Primary School

The Moon

The moon's light and bright.
It smells like cream.
It's dark and I am scared.
It gives me the creeps.
I hear scary noises -
It's crashing and smashing.
It started to get cold.
I've got the shivers!

Leah Riley (8)
Muthill Primary School

Sunshine

Sunshine makes me feel happy,
Not angry since it sparkles in the light,
It sparkles in dark,
Letting people get tanned.
No matter what colour of silky skin,
Shining so bright shines the golden sun!

Karen McCulloch (9)
Muthill Primary School

Storm

I see trees falling like Brazilian rainforest
I hear it like smashing cymbals
Smells like burning electricity,
Lightning striking the farmers' silos
I felt scared . . .

William Roberts (9)
Muthill Primary School

The Stormy Night

There is a big stormy night and not a thing to do.
My mum is trying to sell the coo.
I'm trying to see my friends
But they have gone to their Uncle Ben's.
Although my brother's very thin
He is always in a big spin.
I'm really excited about you
But we are not even halfway through.

Duncan McCallum (8)
Muthill Primary School

Thunder Ride

Grey clouds,
Silver sparks coming down from the sky.
Rumbling like gigantic stones.
It smelt very smoky, sandy as well.
I felt pretty brave
When the thunder came down.

Rory Stewart (8)
Muthill Primary School

Sun

Shiny light in the sky
Looks like glistening gold.
Sizzling fire, burning coals.
You can smell hot flames and summer smells
And I am feeling happy and playful.

Nathan Gannon (8)
Muthill Primary School

Flowers

The flowers softly swish and flow.
All day long, colourful and bright in the night sky.
Birds softly go above them going to the flowers.
Rabbits sleep beside the flowers.
In the morning the sun comes out.
Again the flowers start to shine.
They smell like sweet perfume.
I feel happy.

Rachael Haddow (8)
Muthill Primary School

Moonlight!

The glitzing moon in the woods,
Looks dark and foggy,
Wind blows very smoothly,
Owls hoot at each tree,
Smells like wet wood,
What was that noise?

Katy Scott (8)
Muthill Primary School

Silver Moon

The silver moon shines like a silver spoon
Trees are swishing back and forward
I smell sweet cream
I hear owls tu-whit tu-whooing
The moon is as bright as gold
the wind blows loudly
I feel calm and relaxed
The birds are singing.

Sarah Rattray
Muthill Primary School

Storm And Rain

I see the storm coming, I run.
I bang, bang, bang,
Crash cars bang.
I am scared and terrified and frightened,
I smell mud, poo, smelly.

Alexander Carpenter (9)
Muthill Primary School

Silver Snow

She is cold
She looks like painted white fields.
Thick icing sugar scattered across the land.
Holly rustling in the background.
A robin is singing on a thick, icy branch,
It smells of fresh air that's flown over from the mountains.
Carts of cold air are being swept across your cheek,
Her cold snow through your feet.

Amy Grant (8)
Muthill Primary School

Sleeping Silent

I see thunder and raindrops dropping from the sky,
It looks like a flower in the sky.
I hear the crashing and smashing, even pattering while I sleep,
I smell smoky water and custard,
I feel sleepy as I silently look out the window.

Natasha Gill (8)
Muthill Primary School

Crashing Storm

Crashing storm is rumbling and smashing really loud,
With big black clouds,
Rain falling down and I wonder what is happening in the sky.
It sounds like smashing cymbals,
Everywhere.

Mae Mackay (7)
Muthill Primary School

Snowy Day

Snowy day
Freezing wind
I was feeling happy because it was snowing
Still snowing and I am outside
The flakes fall out of the sky
Cold and beautiful, the snowflakes are white
A bad stormy day.

Claire Gadsby (8)
Muthill Primary School

Twister

Thrashing lightning,
Smashing thunder, crashing rain.
Fallen trees.
Tumbling electrical posts in the deep water.
I see crashing boulders.
I smell flames in the twister.
I smell dust from the rocky hills.
I ran as fast as I could.
I ran into a cave.
I feel scared.

Kieran Allan (9)
Muthill Primary School

The Stormy Night

Crashing thunder is hitting the ground
So hard there are cracks everywhere.
It is killing creatures all around the forest
And it is frightening people, scaring people.
It is horrible, there is something that wants to kill us all,
Beware!

Katie Murray (8)
Muthill Primary School

Midnight Storm

Rain smashing against the ground
A tornado spinning like a spinning top in a faraway land
The only sound you can hear is thunder
It smells of burning
I feel scared, things like trees and roofs are flying through the air.

Corey Boyle
Muthill Primary School

Love

Love is pink,
Love is like a heart.
It sounds like heaven.
It tastes like candyfloss.
It smells like scented roses.
It looks like sweets.
It feels like a *big* cuddle.
It reminds me of my family.

Semone Butt (9)
Our Lady's Primary School

Darkness

Darkness is black.
Darkness is like a spooky cave.
It sounds like a wolf howling.
It tastes like rubbish.
It smells like fish.
It looks dark.
It feels like gunge.

Aidan Stewart (9)
Our Lady's Primary School

Anger

Anger is red.
Anger is like hell.
Anger sounds like a crackling fire,
Anger tastes like hot fire.
Anger smells like burning flesh.
And cracking bones.
Anger looks red.
Anger feels bad.
Anger reminds me of the Devil.

Daniel Buxey (9)
Our Lady's Primary School

Love

Love is pink.
Love is like angels in Heaven.
It sounds like a magic harp.
It tastes like candyfloss.
It smells like sweet sugar.
It looks like a bright sunny day.
It feels like happiness in my heart.
It reminds me of my family.

Tara Hunter (9)
Our Lady's Primary School

Laughter

Laughter is yellow.
Laughter is like jiggling and giggling.
It sounds like a triangle.
It tastes like sweets.
It smells like an air freshener.
It looks like a smile on your face.
It feels like fresh air.
It reminds me of happy days.

Ciara O'Brien (8)
Our Lady's Primary School

Laughter

Laughter is yellow,
Laughter is like there's a tickle in your tummy.
It sounds like a triangle.
It tastes like candy.
It smells like fresh air.
It looks like a smile on your face.
It feels like your mouth will not stop opening.
It reminds me of when my friends make me laugh.

Jade Colvin (8)
Our Lady's Primary School

Laughter

Laughter is multicoloured.
Laughter is a tingling feeling in your mouth.
It sounds like a choir singing.
It tastes like chocolate buns.
It smells like a lovely air freshener.
It looks like a big smile on your face.
It feels like a happy, joyful feeling.
It reminds me of happiness that makes me smile.

Katherine Coyle (9)
Our Lady's Primary School

Anger

Anger is a red colour like the flames of a blazing fire.
It sounds like the screeching of a car tyre skidding along the kerb.
It tastes like burning metal and lava mixed together.
It smells like a horrible rotten body.
It feels like a maggot chewing its way through your skin.
It looks like the Twin Towers crashing to the ground.
It is like a raging war that turns into a massacre.
It sounds like a volcano, *crash!*
And a hurricane, *bang!*
And a tidal wave, *shhh!*
And a rattle snake - rattling its tail.
And a bomb, *boom!*
It does a horrible thing to your body.
It affects others to see you angry
Because you will lash out at people and everything.

Jordan Moore (10)
Our Lady's Primary School

Anger

Anger is red, like flaming red hair
Like a burning fire
Anger is the most vile substance on Earth.
Smelling of burning smoke.
It feels like a burning fire.
It's Hell and I'm in it.
It's frustration eating away at me, causing the most painful agony.
Annoyance, burning hell fire.
It's a raging war where the battle never ends.
Scream!

Anam Qadar (11)
Our Lady's Primary School

Bored

Bored is black like an empty dark street,
It sounds like a howling wolf on the hills
And it tastes like sprouts.
Smells of onions.
A hard rock.
Looks like cats sleeping in the bins.
Bats, bins and dark streets.
An empty forest with trees and no nature.
Yawn!

Ross Peters (10)
Our Lady's Primary School

Calm On A Summer's Morning

Calm is lilac, like a quiet time.
Like birds singing on a summer's morning.
The feeling is like grapes, very sweet.
Calm smells like flowers in your garden.
A humming sound in the open air.
Looking like a duckling with its mother on a pond.
Soft delicate yellow.
Peaceful violins playing a soft tune.

Rosie Hanlon (11)
Our Lady's Primary School

Excited

Excitement is orange, like a burning fire.
It sounds like a big huge chanting crowd
It tastes like a glass of freezing cold water
And smells like wood burning in a forest.
It's like someone surfing on a twenty foot wave.

Martin Gray (11)
Our Lady's Primary School

Brave

Brave is brown, like a thousand bulls.
It sounds like ten lions roaring for freedom.
It tastes like many spices at once.
Smells like a burning fire.
It feels like a burning radiator.
Looking like one man alone in a war.
Fearless bulls battling furiously
A furious bull
Smash!

Kieran Kane (10)
Our Lady's Primary School

Happiness

Happiness is yellow like the bright sunshine
It sounds like bees buzzing and laughter
Luscious ice cream and sweets
It smells like a summer's day
Feels like fresh air
It looks like people smiling and laughing.

Laura Batchelor (11)
Our Lady's Primary School

Worry

Worry is black, like being down in the dumps.
It's like heavy winds.
It's bitter, sour.
Smells of cut grass.
Like a bang on a door.
Looking like a big plane crashing down.
Red, annoyance, irritated and lonely.
Apprehensive time in your life.
Scream!

Jessica Heymans (11)
Our Lady's Primary School

The Weather

I like to splash in the puddles,
Splashing in the rain,
Splashing in the darkness
When it's time to go in.
In the morning when it's bright and breezy,
It's sunny and lovely and playful and quiet,
And the sky is blue.

Katie Purdie (7)
Straloch Primary School

Strathardle Burn

There was a burn runnin' doon Strathardle Glen,
But one day there wis a terrible
Thunder and lightening storm
And it rained aa day.
The burn rose up till it wis awa oot intae the parks.
The burn wis aboot ten metres deep,
And the sheep nearly got drooned.

Sandy Horne (10)
Straloch Primary School

The Cat Family

Lions in tae jungle, walking up an doon,
A little bit like tigers in tae afternoon.
Some little monkeys swinging by the tree,
Ooopsy doopsy tae jaguar eat it far tea
And that's for taeday.

Jessica Purdie (9)
Straloch Primary School

The Weather

Floods, floods that's all we get,
Floods, floods and lots of mud.
Rain, rain
Mud, mud - that's all we get,
To make floods.

Freya Hunter (7)
Straloch Primary School

The Trees

The wind blows the trees,
And the thunder and lightning
Can break the trees.
A chainsaw can break trees as well.
A tree can break another tree.

Matthew Michie (7)
Straloch Primary School

The Weather

The rain is cold
The rain is blue,
But the sun is hot
It's yellow too.
Thunder is noisy,
Lightning scary,
Hailstones are white,
Hailstones are sore
When they come tumbling on your head.

Alaine Michie (8)
Straloch Primary School

Clunskie

Up and doon the Clunskie hull,
Roon a sheep wie the dug,
When I gie thum their feed,
I gae hame for a cup o' tea,
And a cake or twa.

Callum Michie (10)
Straloch Primary School

Guy Fawkes

Glowing
oUtstanding
  Yelling

  Firework night is here
cAtherine
    Wheels and
  rocKets of
      Excitement,
        Sparks of joy.

Jonathan Marshall (11)
The Community School Of Auchterarder

School

S chool is a safe place,
C hildren come to learn,
H oping that they will have lots of fun.
O ver all, they have a good day.
O utside they get to play,
L earning is good fun.

Kayleigh Thom (11)
The Community School Of Auchterarder

World War II

There once was a war called World War II.
They all said they knew what to do.
They heard a loud bell and went for their lunch,
But then all you heard was crunch, crunch, crunch!
'Oh no, the invasion!' somebody said.
More bells could be heard, somewhere outside.
From village to village panic was heard,
Even more panic and people were scared.
The war was so close,
But they had to lose.
So until next time -
We will be fine.

Alan Park (10)
The Community School Of Auchterarder

The Community School Of Auchterarder

A uchterarder is a hard-working school.
U seful children sitting, learning and excelling.
C onstructive looking teachers, teaching good things,
H igh school is like Heaven to everyone.
T errific towns filled with smiling people.
E ncouragement is not needed, it is there.
R ocketing through all correct work.
A ccurate marking and beautifully neat work.
R apidly flying through the work as if it is too easy.
D oing division like hungry lions hunting a deer.
E xceeding work on the neon looking walls.
R esponsible children who are as quiet as a spy.

Ross Dougan (11)
The Community School Of Auchterarder

Hallowe'en

Hallowe'en had arrived,
Ghosts and ghouls were giving everyone a surprise.
Scaring all the children in town,
Taking them all to the planet they'd found
All the adults hiding away,
Very scared in case they got taken away.

The ghosts and ghouls came back to haunt,
From their planet they call Talk-A-Lot.
The ghosts and ghouls invited some friends,
They had a party and enjoyed themselves,
They had their music blasting all night long.
When the party was over
They went back to their planet and brought all the children back,
Their mums were glad, you can count on that.

Nicola Docherty (10)
The Community School Of Auchterarder

A Warm Welcome To Summer

I love it when it's summer
And the dogs get dumber
In the winter it's loads more glummer
The tingling warm sensation is funner
Than the miserable cold.

The sun shines like a block of gold
And paper aeroplanes you have to fold
Melting ice lollies you have to hold
'Come in now,' the children were told.
The final part of summer has come, it's cold.

Emma MacLaren (11)
The Community School Of Auchterarder

My Hamster

S oft and white
A nd cuddly and cute
N early always active
D readfully smart
Y ou should see her.

Robert Main (10)
The Community School Of Auchterarder

Friendship

Friendship is yellow like the sunshine
It feels like happiness
It tastes like chocolate
It looks like people laughing
It sounds like laughing
It smells like sweets
It reminds me of having lots of friends,
Being there for you.

Eilish Syme (9)
The Community School Of Auchterarder

Love

Love is pink like a summer flower.
It tastes like chocolate.
It looks like a heart.
It sounds like a robin.
It smells of a rose.
It feels like a furry cat.
It reminds me of my friends.

Siobhan McKillop (9)
The Community School Of Auchterarder

Summer

S unny days and nights
U ntil it gets to winter
M ilkshakes lying on the ground
M ars bar wrappers all around
E veryone is playing outside on this lovely day
R unning about outside, come on it's fun.

D ays left in the summer holidays
A ll the fun is nearly over
Y achting in the sea
S ummer is such fun.

A re they going to end soon?
R unning round in circles, having water fights.
E ndless fun in the summer holidays.

F inding fish in the river,
U mbrellas gone all dusty because no one has used them,
N ow they are done.

Cameron Smith (11)
The Community School Of Auchterarder

School

I wake up in the morning light
with feelings not at all too bright.
We learn the meaning of the word munch,
and then it's nearly time for lunch.
We learn things all through the day
and yet there still is time to play.
Well I have something to tell you
to me nothing's better than school.

Caroline Harrison (11)
The Community School Of Auchterarder

The Haunted House

As I made my way through the dusty old room,
I couldn't see a thing for the gloom.
I knew they were around,
Making no sound.
Planning to jump out and get me by the light of the moon.

Then I heard something like a cackle of a witch,
The door creaked open but only by a twitch.
Here they come -
So I'd better run
Because they're pulling tricks, just for fun.

I ran and I ran through every door,
There was a lot of cracks and bloodstains on the floor.
Then I came to the Great Hall,
It was the worst room of them all.
If the sight wasn't enough to kill you of fright,
It would definitely keep you up all through the night.

It was the ghouls' grand feast,
It was a gruesome sight as they stuffed their face full of beast.
The smell was dreadful,
The sound was horrific,
They gobbled it up, every single last bit.

As the table was cleared and the lights were turned out,
They put on their music but I still had my doubts.
They asked me to dance,
I ran off in fright,
I galloped away into the darkness of the night.

Then I woke up, I was staring the teacher in the eye,
My face looked puzzled because I didn't know why,
Then it finally clicked, I'd been daydreaming all day,
I knew that there had to be a logical way.
There had been no such thing as witches or ghouls,
It had all been my imagination as I sat there at school.

Samantha Sinclair (11)
The Community School Of Auchterarder

Bonfire Night

Bonfire Night always gives you a fright,
When colours explode in the sky.

Fireworks burst in the sky,
Whilst sparklers sizzle below.

Children scream and shout,
And fill the air, without a doubt.

Adults stand and drink some wine,
Whilst kids run around and have free time.

I just stood there amazed,
Then I shook my head and said, 'They're great!'.

As everybody got up to leave
I felt a wet breeze.

I looked up into the high, dark sky,
I felt a drop of rain.

Kirsty Urquhart (10)
The Community School Of Auchterarder

School

S chool is where I go each day of the week,
C an't do some of the things there.
H ope we do maths today
O nly I don't want to do writing.
O ut of twenty, I got eighteen.
L earning is fun!

Monica Smith (10)
The Community School Of Auchterarder

Germ Invasion

Out of your nose the disgusting stuff flows,
The germs come out like shooting stars.

Falling like leaves, that come off the trees,
They hit the ground, like heavy bars.

All of them whine, this is the third time,
That they've hit their heads hard on the floor.

They stand up to see, on the back of a flea,
That they're in a large department store.

They all salute, their backpacks brimming with loot,
They're ready and raring to go,

The flea puts on his jumping boots,
The general's trumpet makes several hoots,
They're going to put on quite some show.

The flea makes a *leap,* it's over five feet,
As it heads towards the café.

There's bustling and disruption,
Chaos without interruption,
It's busy because it's Saturday.

They land on a tray with one large soufflé,
And the germs hide inside the small holes.

They lie inside, waiting for prey,
They lurk around, it's where they stay,
Who will eat this soufflé?
Nobody knows!

They're into the mouth, they're heading south,
On they go to the organs and knees!

This is a dream, down the bloodstream,
It's is going to be one, great seize!

The person starts to quiver, wriggle and shiver,
Then out come the good bacteria!
Who would have thought, that germs would rot
In one small cafeteria!

They've eaten the inside and rotted the outside,
They've even poisoned the bone marrow!

But the good bacteria are triumphant, joyful and rampant,
It's now time for sleep and on to tomorrow!

Matthew Gordon (11)
The Community School Of Auchterarder

The Ghost Who Wanted To Play

Into the old house I went
That's where I saw a small air vent
In there I saw some eyes look at me!
So I turned around and began to flee
Down the corridor and around the bend
Would this horrid dream ever end?
Then I stopped and turned around
There was crying coming from the ground!
I bent and looked down the hall
Where I saw something get out of the ground and go into the wall
After that it came back out
It was a ghost, barely bigger than a garden sprout.
I recognised its eyes from the air vent
So I asked it to lead me to the exit and I would follow where it went,
It did what I asked, I was grateful too
I stepped outside and the little ghost said, 'Goodbye, I'll miss you,'
And vanished.

Lisa Mackie (10)
The Community School Of Auchterarder

My Hopes And Feelings As An Old Woman

Sitting in my rocking chair,
Thinking about life and
My darling grandchildren.

Oh how my love for them
Is unbreakable.

Missing their sweet innocent faces
Their intelligent minds.

So many options
To choose in life.

All night and all day
I pray for them to make
The right choices.

Too soon it will be their turn
To look back on their lives . . . !

Jordan Cooper (11)
The Community School Of Auchterarder

Space

Outside the Earth's atmosphere,
There's a world that goes on forever.
Full of stars and planets,
And balls of gas that fly around.

It's like a sea of black, that stretches wide,
It does not stop but keeps going on.
There is still more for us to discover,
Because space is like a big blank cover.

Natalie Kerr (10)
The Community School Of Auchterarder

The Magic Pen

I recall one night
I was relaxing on my bed
A wizard came in through the blinds
And said his name was Ned!

I asked him what he wanted
I fainted there and then
Now I know what happened
He stabbed me with his pen!

I guess I learned a lesson
A valuable one too
always keep your blinds shut
Or he will come to you!

Sarah Balfour (11)
The Community School Of Auchterarder

Different Fireworks

Millions of different
fireworks, some *immense,*
some teeny.
Kids playing with sparklers and
writing their names in
the air.
Shooting stars *spreading* across the sky,
some going bang, boom!
Babies screaming from *explosions*
in the air.
They are all gone, so we'll
have to wait till next year!

Louise McPhillimy (10)
The Community School Of Auchterarder

My Hopes And Dreams

I fear the day when I will wake
And be old, wrinkly, sore
But hope for a day
When at Christmas
The snow would be thick on the ground
But soft and easy to move through
With my grandchildren I could play
Make snowmen and snow angels
Have a snowball fight
But after that I would fear
Going to an old folk's home
Then dying
Without knowing.

Ryan Simpson (11)
The Community School Of Auchterarder

Waiting

It's a busy day
I listen to the sirens
Rushing to an emergency
I think of the days
When I was young and played on deserted streets
Watching in awe as a police car rushed past
But now . . .
I just sit alone in my tattered old armchair
Knitting jumpers.
Watching my colourless television
And waiting patiently, in my boring life
For my time to come.

Rachel Pirie (10)
The Community School Of Auchterarder

Feelings

Childhood's past
Old age has come,
Bald and *wrinkled* like a prune
No more mop-like hair
Or velvety skin.
My furniture
Old and dusty,
I sit quietly like a mouse
On my own.
Thinking of my active, wild youth
My old, flaky grandfather clock
Ticks loudly in the corner of
My old dusty living room.
Tick, tick, tick!
Childhood is past
Old age now.

Liam Smith (11)
The Community School Of Auchterarder

The Elderly

The weak elderly sit in
their creaking rocking chairs
rocking to and fro.

Talking slowly about
their pleasant past times
which they miss so much.

Sitting there, quietly wishing
that they could be -
Young again.

Thinking noiselessly about
their long lives.
Do they regret?

Kelsey Watson (11)
The Community School Of Auchterarder

Feelings

The woodworm are slowly killing
My very last pieces of furniture.
My skin feels dry, gasping for air,
A shiver goes around the room,
Tickles my feet
Up my legs and back.
I shudder.
Nearing the end,
Forgotten,
Slowly, heavily, running away
From the world.

The only sound
To comfort me
Is the washing machine
Rumbling in the kitchen.
Feeling angry, I know
The other side is sucking my soul . . .
Away from me.

David C Lawrence (10)
The Community School Of Auchterarder

What's It Like To Be Old

Waking up is a challenge in itself,
Just managing to make my way out of bed.
Feeling my way to the clothes cupboard
Pulling the cord for help,
Being dressed and guided
To the dining hall.
I am seated for breakfast,
Cutting up food
Is another challenge of being blind.

I fear I am at Death's door
And that the day of my death
Is drawing nearer.

Eleanor Gibson (11)
The Community School Of Auchterarder

Hopes And Fears Of An Old Person

Looking at the world now
I see myself
Moving unsteadily upstairs

Looking out and seeing young couples fighting
Thinking they're young and have got something special
But they waste their precious time by arguing.

I would have done anything
To swap lives with one of them.

Back in my day there was only that one special person
Everything has changed now.

Not much point in going on with life now
Everything has to come to an end.

It won't be long now
Till my turn.

Kathryn Robertson (10)
The Community School Of Auchterarder

What It Is Like To Be Old!

I sit on my rocking chair alone,
Silent as the night-time
Switch on the TV to break the silence.
Two actors talking to each other,
Feeling tired.

Hobbling up to my room
As cold as the Arctic up there.
Struggling to change into my ripped, torn pyjamas.
Unsteadily I climb into my creaky old bed.
Violently I pull at my uncomfortable, holey covers.
All alone
I drift into sleep
My time here is nearly up!

Charlotte O'Neill (11)
The Community School Of Auchterarder

My Hopes And Fears

Sitting on my musty old armchair
Hoping
That Death's door
Is far, far away
Fearing
That I am becoming
Like a hermit crab
Cowering into my shell
Desperately alone
Nobody loves me
Creased and deeply furrowed skin
Fading memory
Childhood memories slowly slipping away
Feeling worthless
Feeling unimportant
Wishing I was young again.

Ciaran Anderson (11)
The Community School Of Auchterarder

Being Old

Old and weak
Wrinkles
All over my face
I look in the mirror
I can't look!
It's disgusting
So many -
I'm horrified
I
   Step
      Away.

Hollie Park (10)
The Community School Of Auchterarder

Being Old

I sit on my own
Rocking back and forth
On the old squeaky rocking chair.
Outside, children *shouting*
The phone starts to ring
Picking up
The old tatty walking stick
With my wrinkled hands
I hobble to the
Kitchen to answer it.

Night is dawning once more
I take my medication
Then slowly put on old striped pyjamas.
I climb into bed carefully
And finally
        fall
          asleep.

Nicolle Moffat (11)
The Community School Of Auchterarder

Grampa's Hopes And Fears

Sitting in my rocking chair,
Humming a little tune
A shrivelled old prune,
Thinking
What will life be like
When I'm gone?
I'm old
I'm ancient,
My time is nearly up.

Rachel Parr (11)
The Community School Of Auchterarder

Being Old

Scary thoughts,
Lonely.
Hard of hearing,
Children outside, shouting and screaming.
I think about when
That was me!
A long time ago.
Me, sitting here
On the old wooden chair,
By the cosy, warm fire.
When I'm sitting here
The good feelings come.
I still have some time left
So I'll use it well.

Gemma Mallis (11)
The Community School Of Auchterarder

Great Granny

Great Granny
Old, wrinkled
Like a prune
House small and cosy
Living room cosy, like a woollen jumper
Kitchen yellow like a sunflower

Great Granny
Old, wrinkled
Alone, scared
Wants someone
Around the house
Knock
Knock
Knock!
Who's there?

Louise Docherty (10)
The Community School Of Auchterarder

Love Is Red Like A Rose

It tastes like a bowl of sugar
It looks like they have met at the mall
It sounds like birds singing in the hollow tree
It smells like the redness of a rose
It feels like you're walking on the sea
It reminds me of a big bright heart
Lighting my life as I move on.

Emma McNamara (9)
The Community School Of Auchterarder

Hopes And Fears

My great granny
Reminds me of a raisin
Moving her hand shakily
As though she was scared
Always talking about her childhood
Once she was very good at
Gardening
We would walk for ages
In her beautiful garden.

Kevin Gorlas (11)
The Community School Of Auchterarder

Friendship

Friendship is dark and light like night and day
It tastes like sweets
It looks like you're the only people on Earth
It sounds like people laughing
It smiles like roses in the sun
It feels like you are at the beach
It reminds me of friends staying with you
And sometimes looking after you.

Ashley Docherty (8)
The Community School Of Auchterarder

I Am Old

I'm old
Older than a tree
I sit in my old wooden rocking chair
Creak, creak
Creak, creak

The nurses in the home
Have black eyes, they've been up all night
They're helping an old man
To get him into a wonky wheelchair

Creak, creak
Creak, creak

Everyone else in the home
Is watching the old black and white fuzzy TV
With blank eyes . . .

Freya Bachell (10)
The Community School Of Auchterarder

Being Old

Sitting thoughtfully
by the blazing crackling fire
wishing . . .
wishing . . .
I could run again
play games
dance.
Wishing so hard
my head hurts,
I want to be *outside*
in that *glorious* sunshine
to play all day
till the end.

Amy Ross (11)
The Community School Of Auchterarder

The Day Of An Old Person

They sit old, wrinkled and lonely
on tattered patterned chairs.
Staring tearfully around quiet empty rooms,
sitting in silence.
They read long, tiring, tragic newspapers.

When glowing silver stars appear,
they hobble slowly upstairs.
Struggle to pull on
baggy stained pyjamas.
Slowly slide onto creaking beds.
Then wonder if they will
see the dawn of tomorrow.

Lucy C Menzies (10)
The Community School Of Auchterarder

Funky Friends

F antastic
U nderstanding
N ever nasty
K ind and helpful
Y oung

F unky
R eliable
I ndependent
E ntertaining
N ice friendship
D angled together
S pecial friends.

Hazel Clark (10)
The Community School Of Auchterarder

Hate

It tastes like blood
It smells like darkness
It looks like lightning
It sounds like drums
It feels like lava
It reminds me of Barbie

Alex Kitch (9)
The Community School Of Auchterarder

Silence

Silence is silver like the snow,
It tastes like hard icicles,
It looks like the blue ocean.
It sounds like soft snowballs hitting the ground.
|t feels like smooth slippery snow.
It smells like the coldness in the air.
It reminds me of winter coldness.

Reon Lewis (9)
The Community School Of Auchterarder

Hate

Hate is red, like dripping blood
It tastes like rich chocolate sauce
It looks like darkness in an attic
It sounds like a wolf howling
It smells like a dustbin
It feels like touching fire
It reminds me of people dying.

Jamie Lawrence (8)
The Community School Of Auchterarder

Excitement

It looks like your friend making-up with you,
It tastes like bitter-sweet.
It smells like a sunflower sitting in the garden.
It sounds like birds whistling on a branch.
It feels like running up a hill with a kite in my hand.
It reminds me of my cousin being born.

Alicia Low (8)
The Community School Of Auchterarder

Silence

Silence is silver like the winter snow's hitting the ground,
It tastes like ice melting.
It looks like falling icicles.
It sounds like ice-cold waves flowing.
It smells like ice-cold waters.
It feels like snowballs falling to the ground.
It reminds me of the nice fresh air, outside.

Eilidh Sinclair (9)
The Community School Of Auchterarder

Winter Air

When the winter breeze blows
It makes you feel happy,
When the cold air blows through your hair
And the soft winter snow lands on your face.
It makes your face feel nice and soft
Lying in the soft wet snow
Making angels and having fun.
Opening the presents you got from Santa.

Neil Stewart (11)
The Community School Of Auchterarder

Football

Football sounds like fun
Football tastes like glory
Football smells like victory
Football feels like success
Football looks like a *goaaal!*
Football reminds me of 25/9/04
Rangers vs Moscow.

Josh Goold (9)
The Community School Of Auchterarder

Love

Love is red like shiny, delicious strawberries.
Love feels special and trustful.
Love tastes like romance.
Love looks pretty and romantic.
Love sounds romantic.
Love reminds me of when I was in Greece
Looking at the sunset.

Emily Dewar (9)
The Community School Of Auchterarder

Friendship

Friendship is bright yellow like shiny yellow roses,
It looks like you've made loads of friends to play with
It smells like honeysuckle,
It feels like you're lying down in the sun,
It tastes like golden nuts,
It sounds like a sunbird singing.
It reminds me of leaving Tenerife.

Georgina Shepherd (9)
The Community School Of Auchterarder

Love

Love is red like a red rose
Love sounds of joy
Love tastes of food
Love looks like roses
Love feels big, nice and gentle
Love reminds me of my family.

Kathleen McRostie (9)
The Community School Of Auchterarder

Happiness Is . . .

Happiness is the rainbow
Sounds like caramel bubbling
Tastes like a home-made muffin
Smells like a lovely red rose
Feels like warm brushed fur
Looks like multicolours shooting through the sky
Reminds me of a sizzling hot summer.

Heather Forsyth (10)
The Community School Of Auchterarder

Darkness Is . . .

Darkness is black
Darkness sounds like screaming
Darkness tastes like dark chocolate
Darkness smells like smoke
Darkness feels like a wet wall or bars
Darkness looks like a dark sky with no stars
Darkness reminds me of a prison.

Joshua Watters (10)
The Community School Of Auchterarder

Laughter

Laughter is pink like shiny newborn piglets
It tastes like licky tangy liquorice,
It sounds like funny children playing.
It feels like a soft cuddly teddy bear.
It looks like cheery little people,
It reminds me of Dick and Dom in da bungalow.

Amy Wilkie (9)
The Community School Of Auchterarder

Joy

Joy is yellow like the bright yellow sun,
It feels like lots of fun and laughter.
It smells like lots of fresh air.
It tastes like fresh orange juice.
It sounds like people laughing.
It looks like people having fun.
It reminds me of having lots of fun.

Andrew Langdown (8)
The Community School Of Auchterarder

My Friend

My friend has a cousin who has a friend who has a mum.
Her mum has a friend whose mum has a cat.
The cat has a flea and the flea doesn't know anybody
So the poem ends here!

Katie Langlands (9)
The Community School Of Auchterarder

Loneliness

The colour of loneliness is green.
The taste of loneliness is metal.
The sound of loneliness is people saying, 'Goodbye'.
The smell of loneliness is damp.
The feel of loneliness is unspeakable.
Loneliness looks like nobody.
It reminds me of nothing.

Ruby Cumming (9)
The Community School Of Auchterarder

Peace

The war is over
The peace is yet to come
It's clear skies from here on.
People are relieved
After people have grieved.
The weapons are put down
The peace has been taken up.

Peter Scott (10)
The Community School of Auchterarder

Joy

Joy is orange like the piercing hot sun.
It tastes like a ripe, juicy orange.
It smells like melted chocolate just out of the oven.
It looks like toast with a lot of melted butter.
It sounds like someone opening a can of Fanta.
It feels like something bubbling inside you.
It reminds me of my birthday and Christmas.

Miranda Radley (8)
The Community School of Auchterarder

Love

Love is pink like blossom in the sun.
It tastes like sweet strawberries.
It looks like pink blossom.
It sounds like someone playing the harp.
It smells like strawberries.
It feels like happiness in the air.
It reminds me of love moments.

Lisa Welsh (9)
The Community School of Auchterarder

Sadness

Sadness is like . . .

It tastes like poison in your mouth
It feels like a big weight on your shoulders
It looks like blue paint in your hand
It sounds like a very low drum
It smells like a gas
It reminds me of darkness.

Gary Gilmartin (8)
The Community School of Auchterarder

Silence

Silence is blue like a cold winter's morning
It looks like an icicle falling to the ground
It smells like fresh air
It tastes like icy snow
It feels like cold water
It reminds me of a dark night.

Calum Zielinski (9)
The Community School of Auchterarder

Love Is . . .

Love is pink like an apple blossom tree
It tastes like you're sucking a sweet
It feels like you're hot and sweaty
It looks like Cupid's arrow with pink flowers
It smells like summer's bounty
It reminds me of running in fields
It sounds like romantic music.

Marcus Mollison (9)
The Community School of Auchterarder

Silence

Silence is white like the cold ice
It tastes like the thin air
It looks like see-through jelly
It sounds like rain pattering down
It smells like freezing water
It reminds me of total peace.

Kieran Smith (8)
The Community School of Auchterarder

Sadness

Sadness is blue like an ocean of tears falling down your cheek.
It tastes like tears from the ocean of tears.
It feels like water dripping down your cheek.
It looks like blue drops of water dripping down.
It sounds like blue rain dropping on your window.
It smells like a salty ocean of tears.
It reminds me of blue drops of rainy tears.

Kimberley McPhee (9)
The Community School of Auchterarder

Friendship

Friendship is silver like a bestfriend's necklace.
It looks like children laughing and playing.
It tastes like black cherry.
It sounds like voices and laughter.
It feels like someone who is always there.
It smells like ripe strawberries.
It reminds me of love hearts.

Lucy O'Neill (8)
The Community School of Auchterarder

Friendship

Friendship is yellow like a star.

It looks like you are having fun.
It feels like you are a good friend.
It sounds like fun.
It smells like something sweet.
It tastes like some sweet sugar.
It reminds me of happy moments.

Mikaela Benett (9)
The Community School of Auchterarder

Love

Love is red like roses.
It looks like a beautiful love heart in someone's arms.
It tastes like a red, shiny apple with a love heart bite out of it.
It sounds like romantic love music on a CD player.
It smells like perfume in a red, small box.
It feels like your heart is bubbling.
It reminds you of your first kiss!

Erin Walker (9)
The Community School of Auchterarder

Love

Love is red like a heart.
It tastes like red jelly.
It looks like a red sunset.
It sounds like a red robin.
It smells like a red rose..
It feels like a red, soft toy.
It reminds me of my cousin's red buggy.

Christie Warren (9)
The Community School of Auchterarder

Fear

Fear is red like blood.
It looks like someone is about to die.
It tastes like you don't have friends.
It sounds like voices coming from the ground.
It smells like death is near.
It feels like your friendship is over.
It reminds me of bad things.

Callum Mackie (8)
The Community School of Auchterarder

Love

Love is pink like peach blossom.
It tastes like cherries.
It looks like a heart in your head.
It sounds like some wedding bells.
It smells like a lovely bird.
It feels like a smooth life.
It reminds me of making friends.

Jamie-Lee McLean (9)
The Community School of Auchterarder

Hate

Hate is red like fire.

It tastes like pain.
It feels like blood.
It looks like darkness.
It sounds like someone is coming.
It smells like lava.
It reminds me of tomatoes.

Hamilton Smith (9)
The Community School of Auchterarder

Love

Love is rosy-pink like flowers blossoming in summer.
It tastes like chocolate melting in your mouth.
It smells like Mum's home baking.
It feels like happiness whizzing round me.
It reminds me of love hearts flying in the sky.
It looks like a pearl heart necklace.
It sounds like classical music.

Rebecca Anderson (8)
The Community School of Auchterarder

Hate

Hate is scarlet like runny fluid blood.
It looks like burning fire.
It smells like skeletons and hot ash.
It sounds like screaming in your head.
It tastes like fear and jealousy put together.
It feels like you're about to punch the person you hate.
It reminds me of the devil.

Logan Parr (8)
The Community School of Auchterarder

Darkness

Darkness is black like a dark blackout eclipse.
It looks like you're in a giant blackberry.
It sounds like nothing.
It tastes like a rambler.
It smells like fresh air.
It feels like nothing else is in the world.
It reminds me of going to bed.

Greg Sanders (9)
The Community School of Auchterarder

Laughter

Laughter is white like cold, frosty snow.
It smells like a slimy, burpy toad.
It sounds like someone eating an apple.
It looks like a shiny, iced floor.
It tastes like a melting strawberry ice lolly.
It feels like a heart just been taken out of a man.
It reminds me of a Celt freezing to death.

Rebecca Greig (9)
The Community School of Auchterarder

Hate

Hate is grey like a rumbling, crashing thunder cloud,
It feels uncomfortable, welled up inside,
It smells of jealousy and envy,
It looks like a sour lemon,
It tastes of wriggling worms,
It sounds like cracking knuckles and clenching fists,
It reminds me of hissing vipers.

Annie Booth (8)
The Community School of Auchterarder

Love

Love is red like juicy strawberries.
It feels like your best friends.
It sounds like something beating.
It looks like a sunset over the river.
It smells like chocolate.
It tastes of sweets.
It reminds me of my guinea pig Smudge.

Cheryl Marchbank (8)
The Community School of Auchterarder

Friendship

Friendship is like the shining sea,
Friendship smells like lovely blue autumn flowers,
It tastes like the sunset,
It feels good like making a new friend,
It sounds like a lot of snow falling,
It reminds me of friends who left the school.

Liam Kirk (9)
The Community School of Auchterarder

Eggs

I went in the fridge
I dropped the egg
So did Dad
And Mum
We had to go to the shop again
We tried again
But we did it all over again
No point buying eggs again.

Katie MacFadyen (10)
The Community School of Auchterarder

Excitement

Excitement is green like broccoli.
It looks like dinosaurs.
It smells like green mushy peas.
It tastes like blood.
It feels like an old man.
It sounds like a tap dripping.
It reminds me of my family.

Richard Saffrey
The Community School of Auchterarder

Fear

Fear is black like monsters,
It feels like a damp coldness against your skin,
It looks like yellow eyes looking at you,
It smells like dead people,
It tastes like mud,
It sounds like screams for help,
It reminds me of zombies.

Josh Roy (9)
The Community School of Auchterarder

Happiness

Happiness is like the wonderful green grass
                        and a beautiful blue flower.
Happiness sounds like whooshing water of the sea.
Happiness feels like the softness of tissues.
Happiness looks like the yellow paint of toes.
Happiness smells like perfume.
Happiness tastes like pizza.
Happiness reminds me of a sunny day.

Ewan Burnie (8)
The Community School of Auchterarder

Love

Love is red
Love tastes like sugar
Love looks all red and it's moving all around
Love feels like your tummy going upside down
Love is the time you get to know who loves you
Love is like falling to the ground.

Jacqueline Porteous
The Community School of Auchterarder

Darkness

Darkness is faded blue like blueberries hung from a tree.
It smells like chewed up, rotted fish.
It tastes of bitter cherries.
It feels like dark clouds about to open and rain.
It sounds like a deafening cry from a creature far away.
It looks like a 12 o'clock full moon shining a reflection on the river
Like a pair of red eyes glaring at you
And backing away into the dark shadows.
It reminds me of an old warehouse with dented doors
And cracked and broken windows.

Eliot Short (9)
The Community School of Auchterarder

Fear

Fear is red like burning, hot flames.
Fear smells like cloudy, foggy smoke.
It feels like being swallowed up by a deep, dark hole.
It sounds like scary, strange silence.
It tastes like a sour lemon.
It looks like deep darkness.
It reminds me of a large, black python coiling itself around me.

Calum Dann (9)
The Community School of Auchterarder

Young Writers - Once Upon A Rhyme Tayside

Happiness

Happiness is yellow like the hot sun.
It looks like happiness in people's eyes.
It smells like flowers in the fields.
It tastes like yellow melting ice lollies.
It feels like fresh air.
It sounds like big fun.
It reminds me of all my friends.

Suzanne Porteous (9)
The Community School of Auchterarder

Friendship

Friendship is yellow like a gold, shiny ring.
Friendship sounds like a beautiful bird singing.
It smells like lovely perfume.
It looks like flowers.
It tastes like a fresh strawberry.
It feels like a small, wonderful butterfly.
It reminds me of my best friend Jade.

Mhairi Gorlas (8)
The Community School of Auchterarder

Joy

Joy is like blue poppies.
It looks like happiness.
It sounds like the trees rustling.
It tastes like ice cream.
It feels like conkers.
It reminds me of my family.

Alistair Wood (8)
The Community School of Auchterarder

Love

Love is red like the flaming sun
It looks like a red, red rose
It sounds like a bird singing
It smells like beautiful flowers blossoming in the sun
It tastes like strawberry ice cream
It feels like the hot sun burning
It reminds me of my mum and dad getting married.

Sara Miller (9)
The Community School of Auchterarder

Fear

Fear is pale like a big, lovely plum.
It sounds like a mouse which is too scared to speak.
It feels like something licking you and squirting you with water.
It tastes like you're trapped and only get raw egg to eat.
It looks like everybody is trying to hurt you.
It smells like sweat and you dying.
It reminds me of tiny worms.

Duncan Tait (8)
The Community School of Auchterarder

Hate

Hate is red like a hot, steaming and burning building.
It feels like sticky, hot liquid and bubbly, bulging fire.
It looks like bubbly, bulging, hot and steaming magma.
It sounds like a cat yelping and tornadoes hitting Earth.
It tastes like hot, tangy chilli sauce.
It smells like hot, steamy and choking smoke.
It reminds me of a bite of a black mamba.

Kimberly Russell (9)
The Community School of Auchterarder

Love

Love sounds like music bumping up and down.
Love tastes like nice, juicy, fresh coconuts.
Love smells like a sweet, sweet rose.
Love feels like dipping your hands in cold paint.
Love looks like a lovely black horse cantering in the breeze.
Love reminds me of nice pink candyfloss.

Kessiah Pattenden (10)
The Community School of Auchterarder

Inside My Shed

Inside my shed is a silver bike
Under the wheel is a dead fish called Pike
On the seat is a nibbling hamster
Outside the door is a smelly dumpster.

On top of the freezer is a little train set
Which I won during a bet
I walked across the shed and stood on a screw
And it went right through my new shoe.

Thomas Sinclair (9)
Timmergreens Primary School

Happiness

Happiness is bright colours like yellow,
The taste of happiness is strawberries,
Happiness is the smell of roses all lovely and sweet,
It looks like the sun is shining through,
Happiness sounds like the birds are singing,
Happiness feels like soft things like soft covers and pillows.

Rachel Banks (7)
Timmergreens Primary School

Guess Who? Kennings

Sleep walker
Tea maker
Backgammon player
Kid carer
Hard worker
Chocolate seeker
Good listener
Coffee lover
TV watcher
Hair washer
Book reader
Shopping buyer
House cleaner
Homework helper
Spelling tester

My super duper mother!

Jill Finlayson (10)
Timmergreens Primary School

Guess Who? Kennings

Brilliant runner
Brave chaser
Steady starter
Fast finisher
Healthy eater
Record holder
Avid trainer
Medal wearer
Tom Cruise lover!
Definite winner
British basher

My idol, Kelly Holmes.

Christine McLoughlin (11)
Timmergreens Primary School

Guess Who? Kennings

Girl hater
Friend lover
Football player
Brave darer
Bad dancer
Goal seeker
Lousy dater
Terrible singer
Special sprayer
Floppy dresser
Big bruiser
Hates hairdressers

That's me.

Paul Barber (11)
Timmergreens Primary School

Guess Who? Kennings

Monkey hater
Sweet baker
Football lover
Bad singer
Pants wearer
Neither faker
Lady winner
Big shaker
Good runner
Brilliant hopper
Party lover
Excellent sprinter
Cricket hater
Shoe maker
Paul Barber.

Hugh Stewart (11)
Timmergreens Primary School

Guess Who? Kennings

Mum lover
Brother lover
Speedy crawler
Slow eater
Happy giggler
Loud screamer
Nappy wearer
Dummy sucker
Super dribbler
Juice spiller
Good sleeper
Noise maker

My baby sister.

Conor Howden (9)
Timmergreens Primary School

Guess Who? Kennings

Pizza eater
Fantastic dancer
Fashion wearer
Beautiful teacher
Awful singer
Great laughter
Sweetie giver . . . *mmm*
Hair flicker
Fantasy reader
Big spender
DVD collector
Jazz lover

My favourite teacher, Miss Kerr.

Katie Esplin (10)
Timmergreens Primary School

Guess Who? Kennings

Good runner
Toast burner
Manchester supporter
Bad moaner
Football lover
Annoying brother
Loud shouter
Terrible listener
Trouble maker
Toy breaker
Bad singer

My annoying brother.

Ross Milne (10)
Timmergreens Primary School

Guess Who? Kennings

Football player
Super striker
Brechin supporter
Snickers lover
Job hater
Beer drinker
Quick thinker
Joke maker
Cookie eater
Pocket money giver
Tax payer

My fantastic father!

Evan A Hill (11)
Timmergreens Primary School

Guess Who? Kennings

Football player
Good swimmer
Awful dancer
Man U supporter

Brill cooker
Fast eater
Booze drinker
Pizza maker

Brick lifter
Earth digger
Super painter
Wall builder

My dad.

Kris Duff (11)
Timmergreens Primary School

Guess Who? Kennings

Football player
England winger
Terrible faker
Free kick taker
Big spender
Money maker
Winning wisher
Good winner
Bad loser
Man U betrayer

David Beckham!

Dayle Fowler (11)
Timmergreens Primary School

Guess Who? Kennings

Guitar player
Fast swimmer
Basketball player
Long sleeper
Morning hater
TV lover
Celtic supporter
Coke drinker
Pizza eater
Money maker
Car washer
High jumper
Excellent drawer
Good runner
Bad dancer

That's me.

Paul Reid (11)
Timmergreens Primary School

On My Dinner Plate

On my dinner plate
I'm sure I'll find a lot of toes,
Oh dear! It was just pasta bows.
Is that blood, thick and red?
Nope, it's only tomato sauce instead.
They're fingers from my nana,
No way, it's just banana.
Why is there a wing from a parrot?
So I'm wrong, it's only carrot.
That has to be some bumblebees,
No, it's only cheese!

Lauren Breach (9)
Timmergreens Primary School

Guess Who? Kennings

Great baker
Coffee drinker
Diet doer
Slow eater
Meal maker

Pencil sharpener
Rubber outer
Neat writer
Child carer
Polite helper

Hair straightener
Nail cutter
Medium runner
Coat hater
Umbrella lover

Film liker
Big shopper
Crazy chuckler
Quiet whisperer
Loud shouter

My wonderful mum.

Steven Cadger (11)
Timmergreens Primary School

Fear

Fear is black.
It tastes like frozen mice
And smells like boiled blood.
Fear looks like a walking skeleton,
And sounds like people screaming.
Fear feels like scary ghosts that you cannot touch.

Luke Shepherd (8)
Timmergreens Primary School

Guess Who? Kennings

Tail wager
Sleep hater
Fast runner
Food nicker
Rabbit chaser
Water slurper
Bone eater
Wood chewer
Walk lover
Sofa ripper
Door scratcher
Shoe muncher

My dog.

Hannah Kate Cargill (10)
Timmergreens Primary School

Guess Who? Kennings

Joke lover
Loud speaker
Marvellous finder
Inside hater
Evil hunter
Great helper
Open minder
Outside lover
Dare thinker
Running competitor
Umbrella hater
Money spender

My best friend Jamie Goodrum.

Shane Holt (10)
Timmergreens Primary School

Inside My Teacher's Cupboard

Inside my teacher's cupboard
I'm sure I would find
A dragon, green with red polka dots,
Dungeons with chains to hang boys from,
A bottle of wine, the rarest kind,
A guillotine with a head in a basket,
A hairy tarantula away to bite,
Walls closing in with spikes,
A Celebrations tin full of poisonous sweets,
A witch's broomstick cooling down,
A spellbook on the highest shelf,
Talking pumpkins telling stories.
She let me in her cupboard
And I saw . . .
Paper, jotters, Blu-tack, chalk
And a big bottle of paint.
But at the back I saw
A witch's hat.

Kieran Scott (9)
Timmergreens Primary School

Guess Who? Kennings

Fast runner
Walker lover
Tummy scratcher
Mud roller
Sofa jumper
Rabbit chaser
Bed snatcher
Bone cruncher
Body licker
Water slurper
Tail wagger
Frolic muncher

My dog.

Jamie Goodrum (10)
Timmergreens Primary School

Guess Who

Nice springer
Cute grinner
Fast digger
Trainer nicker
Lovely snapper
Tired napper
Tissue eater
Goal keeper
Running nutter
Grass cutter
Fun maker
Treat taker
Water gulper
She's nice as sulphur
Have you worked it out yet?
No!
Then I guess I'll have to tell you,
It's my dog
Riva!

Beth Johnston (11)
Timmergreens Primary School

Happiness

Bright lilac, pink, peach and yellow are the colours of happiness.
Happiness is the taste of sour sweets and chocolate fudge.
Happiness is the smell of red roses and sweet strawberry ice cream.
Happiness is the sight of blue birds flying in the sky
and the flowers waving in the wind.
Happiness is the sound of birds tweeting in the sky
and laughter of children.
Happiness is the feeling of a furry cushion
and the comfiest bed in the world.

Niamh Hill (7)
Timmergreens Primary School

Guess Who? Kennings

Strong winner
Nice grinner
Lovely hacker
Fast canter
Cheeky chancer
Proud prancer
Neat pacer
Good racer
Big drinker
Greedy eater
But she's always there
If you need her
It's my pony Missy.

Jill Smith (11)
Timmergreens Primary School

Kennings

Brilliant runner
Definite winner
Avid trainer
Healthy eater
Record breaker
Medal chaser
British taker

It is the one and only
Kelly Holmes.

Abbie Stewart (11)
Timmergreens Primary School

Kennings

Cage nibbler
Sleep waker
Best runner
Brilliant eater
Spring reminder
Food finder
Bad climber
Wheel sprinter
Water drinker
This is my hamster Nadia!

Lucy Wishart (10)
Timmergreens Primary School

Inside My Uncle's Shed

Inside my uncle's shed I'm sure that I would find,
A massive tub of hair gel, the gooiest, stickiest kind.
A big wardrobe full of party clothes and glitzy shoes that shine.
A cupboard full of party food, all tasting rather fine.
A disco ball hanging from the roof for a disco in the shed.
An expensive karaoke machine, a hammock for a bed.
A bottle of beer under the sink that he doesn't show his wife.
An Elvis suit behind the door that gives him a new life.
One day he let me in the shed,
It was full of normal things.
A broken lamp, a saw, some wood,
A microwave that pings,
A table that needs mending,
Some sawdust on the floor.
He really is quite normal,
He's really quite a bore.

Toni Tindal (9)
Timmergreens Primary School

Inside My Teacher's Cupboard

Inside my teacher's cupboard
I'm sure I would find
A piece of rice,
Some black and white mice
To chuck in her gloomy cauldron.
But up higher still, on the very top shelf,
A jar with a goblin's eye.
I bet there's another with a label that says,
'For the naughtiest children who lie'.
But at the back there probably are,
Some children screaming in pain.
They might have been hypnotised,
And now they are going insane.
Then one day I was super-good,
So she led me inside by the hand.
As soon as I looked, I fainted and puked,
At the sight of a magic wand.

Alanah Richards (8)
Timmergreens Primary School

Inside My Toy Box

In my toy box lies a half eaten nut
My golf stick is in there because I putt
My dog's squishy toy is broken in two
My old toy cow that used to moo.

My mum's lipstick is in it, it has no lid
My best toy too and he cost two quid
My timetable poster
And my youth club coaster.

Caitlin McLoughlin (9)
Timmergreens Primary School

In The Teacher's Bag

Inside the teacher's bag,
Lies a few little fags.
An old, soft apple left inside,
Ants crawl in and find a place to hide.

A little magazine all scrunched up in a bundle,
Gathering dust about to crumble.
She has bright red lipstick she thinks is stunning,
I think it's icky and it looks like it's running.

Her bright pink eyeshadow leaks all over, making her mad,
It's like a pink explosion that has gone bad.
She also carries a dirty cup,
That holds dirty water and clogs it up.

She also has bits of crumbs, that roll around in gum,
She also has a receipt for a 'Yum yum.'
Nail files, toe clippers, she has it all,
It's like a beauty parlour on call.

She has a timetable that's slightly wrong,
She has a thin ruler that's very long.

Kate Richards (9)
Timmergreens Primary School

Anger

Anger is red like a ferocious fire in my soul.
It sounds like waves crashing against the rocks.
It tastes like a piece of rotten fruit stuck in the back of your throat.
It smells like smoke from a burnt-out fire.
It looks like a lion taking its anger out on a poor defenceless animal.
It feels like a sword stabbing me in the back.
It reminds me of a demolition ball crashing into a building.

Zak Kennedy (10)
Timmergreens Primary School

The Teacher's Bag

In my teacher's bag, a mobile all dusty
And some of it is a bit rusty
Some keys for the door
And much, much more.

Lipstick, bright and red
And a bolt for her bed
In her purse a five pound note
And a fur coat.

At the bottom, a rubber band
Some stones and sand
Nail clippers
And some slippers.

In another pocket there is a hair brush
And some blush
Her favourite black mascara
And a photo of her father.

Mia McQuillan (9)
Timmergreens Primary School

Inside My Bedroom

There lies a brown, shiny violin,
Then a painted purple bin.
My silver metal, shiny bunk bed,
Better than the one in the shed.

When my CD player is blaring,
Out my window my brothers are staring.
In my bedroom lies a bag,
That I got from my favourite mag.

Purple nail polish, one of a kind,
You can see it from behind.
Beautiful cuddly toys,
Some of them are for boys.

Beth Milne (9)
Timmergreens Primary School

Sadness

Sadness is black,
Sadness tastes of a mouldy melon.
It smells like old, dirty muck.
Sadness looks like people that are crying.
Sadness sounds like a sad movie.
Sadness feels like no one is there to take care of you.

Megan Clubb (8)
Timmergreens Primary School

Excitement

Excitement is a light blue,
Excitement tastes like lasagne with extra cheese,
It feels like your conscience bumping about,
It looks like a huge tidal wave
And it sounds like a big, sizzling pan.
Excitement feels like you're tingling right down.

Robert Anderson (8)
Timmergreens Primary School

Loneliness

Loneliness is the colour black,
It smells like sawdust.
Loneliness looks like a dark room,
It sounds like footsteps.
Loneliness feels like a brick.

Kimberley Cadger (8)
Timmergreens Primary School

Anger

Anger makes me feel very red.
It tastes like hot chilli peppers.
It smells like hot lava.
It looks like burning fire.
Anger sounds like trees burning.
Anger feels like the hot sun when it is hot.

Jamie Thomson (7)
Timmergreens Primary School

Happiness

Being happy is light blue.
It tastes like ice cream.
Happiness smells like roses.
Happiness looks like a happy singer
And sounds like some birds singing.
Happiness feels like the beach.

Chloe Churchill (7)
Timmergreens Primary School

Happiness

Happiness is yellow and pink.
It tastes like sweets and pizza
And smells like a lovely rose.
It looks like singing and dancing
And sounds like a nice song.
Happiness feels like a nice, relaxing time.

Erin Stewart (8)
Timmergreens Primary School

Happiness

Happiness is the colour of yellow.
Happiness tastes like hot dogs.
Happiness smells like roses.
Happiness looks like children playing.
Happiness sounds like people laughing.
Happiness feels like a teddy bear.

Luke Mathieson (8)
Timmergreens Primary School

Happiness

The colour of happiness is gold.
The taste of happiness is fruit salad.
It smells like nice flowers.
It looks colourful and beautiful.
It sounds like a bird singing.
It feels quite smooth and soft.

Sean Matthew (8)
Timmergreens Primary School

Happiness

Happiness is the colour pink.
Happiness tastes like sweets.
Happiness smells like a rose.
It looks like a beautiful cake.
It sounds like a bird singing.
Happiness feels like a safe blanket.

Amy Nairn (8)
Timmergreens Primary School

Happiness

Happiness is yellow,
It tastes like hot dogs
And it smells like Ribena.
It looks like a group of friends.
Happiness sounds like giggling.
Happiness feels like the hot sun.

Amber Beaton (8)
Timmergreens Primary School

Happiness

Happiness is the colour of bright red.
The taste of chocolate and ice cream.
Smells like red and blue roses.
Looks like the light part of the sea.
Sounds like wedding bells.
Feels like meeting new friends.

Christopher Barber (9)
Timmergreens Primary School

Happiness

Happiness is the colour purple and pink.
It tastes like ice cream with lots of chocolate sauce.
Happiness smells like melting chocolate.
Happiness looks like flowers growing.
It sounds like people laughing.
Happiness feels like I should skip around the garden.

Madison Randles (8)
Timmergreens Primary School

Happiness

Happiness is yellow.
It tastes like cheese and tomato pizza
And smells like a big bunch of red roses.
It looks like boys on a football pitch.
Happiness sounds like waves splashing.
Happiness feels like a soft baby blanket.

Samuel Nutt (8)
Timmergreens Primary School

Happiness

The colour of happiness is bright red
Happiness tastes of toffee cake
The smell of happiness is sunflowers
It looks like flowers
Happiness sounds like birds singing
Happiness feels like eating an apple.

Cameron Watt (8)
Timmergreens Primary School

Happiness

Happiness is the colour of red and yellow.
It tastes like chocolate and ice cream
And smells like a punnet of strawberries.
It looks like a funfair because you get fun things there.
Happiness sounds like the circus because it is happy music
And feels like me and my friends.

Matthew Hayes-Reekie (8)
Timmergreens Primary School

Anger

Anger is red like a volcano erupting,
It sounds like a bomb exploding,
It smells like an old, smelly gym sock,
It tastes like some lava in my mouth,
It looks like a bubbling potion,
It feels like a charging bull just hit me,
It reminds me of a volcano exploding and destroying a city.

Jordan Crabb (10)
Timmergreens Primary School

Anger

Anger is black, like a black hole in space.
It sounds like the most dangerous hurricane making its way
                                    through a big city.
It tastes like a mouldy, rotten apple about to be eaten by maggots.
It smells like millions of dirty babies' nappies.
It looks like a rotten, dead hand.
It feels like when I broke my wrist.
It reminds me of my dad.

Chantelle McIntosh (10)
Timmergreens Primary School

Anger

Anger is red like a dragon breathing out fire.
Anger is red like a demon's eyes.
It sounds like a demon laughing.
It tastes like burning hot barbecue sauce sizzling in my mouth.
It smells like cows' dung, so bad.
It looks like an angry bull.
It reminds me of a dragon whacking me with his tail.

Allie Marie Allardice (9)
Timmergreens Primary School

Love

Love is pale pink like candyfloss.
It sounds like people laughing and having fun.
It tastes like juicy strawberries with melted chocolate.
It smells like lovely white daisies just grown.
It looks like bright colours from the sun.
It feels like a big, warm, cuddly hug.
It reminds me of my family.

Rachel Watson (10)
Timmergreens Primary School

Happiness

Happiness is yellow like the sunshine blazing down on me.
It sounds like people talking to their friends.
It tastes like vanilla ice cream with strawberry sauce on top.
It smells like red roses and flowers.
It looks like a sunny, smiling face.
It feels like eating chocolate.
It reminds me of playing my music.

Ellie Whyte (10)
Timmergreens Primary School

Love

Love is like red roses falling from the sky,
It sounds like smooth music coming from the radio,
It tastes like chocolate bars,
It smells like lovely red roses,
It looks like love hearts hanging from the ceiling,
It feels like fluffy cushions,
It reminds me of a cosy room full with pink, red and gold candles.

Charlotte Kay (9)
Timmergreens Primary School

Fear

Fear is black like when I'm scared.
It smells like garbage.
It tastes like strong orange cheese.
It looks like a monster in the bedroom.
It sounds like a drum.
It feels like goo.
It reminds me of home, being all alone there.

Alexander O'Brien (10)
Timmergreens Primary School

Hate

It sounds like someone is banging a pot on your head.
It tastes like I have bitten into a sour lemon.
It smells like black smoke from a flickering fire.
It looks like a volcano exploding out of my head.
It feels like a dart being thrown at my heart.
It reminds me of the colour dark red.

Jamie Butler (10)
Timmergreens Primary School

Hate

Hate is dark blue like the sky in winter
It sounds like someone scratching their nails down a blackboard
It tastes like the spiciest curry sizzling in my mouth
It smells like a baby's dirty nappy lying open
It looks like a person shouting at a child because they've been bad
It feels like someone's trying to hurt me by kicking me
It reminds me of someone crying in the corner of a room.

Jade Beaton (10)
Timmergreens Primary School

Anger

Anger is red like a boulder rushing down a mountain
It sounds like thunder crashing
It smells like smoke from my fireplace
It feels like getting an electric shock
It looks like my dad when he is angry
It tastes like a rotten apple
It reminds me of the Dundee volcano.

Corey Watt (10)
Timmergreens Primary School

Love

Love is baby-blue like the lovely blue sky
It smells like lovely red roses from the garden
It sounds like soft and gentle talking
It feels like sitting in front of a hot and cosy fire
It tastes like I am eating hot chocolate cake and it is melting
in my mouth
It looks like other people giving people presents on Valentine's day
It reminds me of my big cousin and her boyfriend.

Amy Mackie (9)
Timmergreens Primary School

Fear

Fear is white like a scared person
It sounds like a bear going wild
It tastes like loads of water in my mouth
It smells like fresh air
It looks like a bunch of people going mad
It feels like dogs' hard bones
It reminds me of Dad twisting my arm.

Nicky Stubbington (9)
Timmergreens Primary School

Love

Love is red like the soft smell of roses
It sounds like the music from Valentine's day playing softly and sweetly
It tastes like the smooth Dairy Milk taste in my mouth
It smells like the soft smell of roses
It looks like the picture in my head of a gigantic heart surrounded
by white doves
It feels like the soft touch of silk on my skin
It reminds me of my heart filling with joy.

Jordan Lamont (9)
Timmergreens Primary School

Anger

Anger is red like a person with steam coming out of their ears.
It sounds like someone raging with anger.
It tastes like the hottest chilli in the world.
It smells like smoke coming from a red-hot, boiling fire.
It looks like when you're down in Hell.
It feels like touching a fully boiled kettle.
It reminds me of a volcano exploding.

Kieran Whitton (9)
Timmergreens Primary School

Anger

Anger is red like a dragon blowing fiery flames
It tastes like red-hot chillies sizzling in my mouth
It smells like my food has gone on fire and I only smell flames
It looks like a dragon blowing red-hot flames
It feels like a little horrible devil in my head
It reminds me about scary movies I have watched.

Ellen Watson (10)
Timmergreens Primary School

Anger

Anger is red like flames upon flames on logs slowly turning to ash.
It feels like getting poked and poked until you let it all out.
It sounds like ferocious waves hitting off sharp, jagged rocks.
It smells like out of date, burnt food.
It tastes like dark black, burnt toast.
It looks like an animal watching a poacher kill some of its family.
It reminds me of a brick wall no one can break down.

Amber Clarke (10)
Timmergreens Primary School

Anger

It sounds like a huge, tremendous, blood-curdling hurricane
It tastes like steak that's been off for months
It smells like a huge, smelly pile of garbage
It looks like a burning stream of oil
It feels like a huge forest of spikes
It reminds me of a scary creature attacking me.

John Simpson (10)
Timmergreens Primary School

Anger

Anger is red and yellow like a blazing fire
It sounds like a volcano
It tastes like a strong bit of cheese
It smells like a smelly sock
It looks like a lion looking right at me
It feels like a dragon chewing my head off
It reminds me of my big sister.

Nicole Allardice (9)
Timmergreens Primary School

Myself

Joel
Kind
Active
Funny
Who wishes to be an archaeologist
Dreams of being able to breathe underwater
Who wonders what it would be like to be a millionaire
Fears of the Earth being destroyed
Likes playing football and scoring
Hates it when Arbroath loses at football
Loves
Food
Football
Family
Plans
To keep being an archaeologist
Travel the world
Go to college
Joel.

Joel Beattie (10)
Timmergreens Primary School

Love

Love is red like love hearts around me.
It sounds like people playing the harp.
It tastes like runny chocolate running down my chin.
It smells like big, luscious red roses.
It looks like a field of big tulips.
It feels like people playing the piano for me.
It reminds me of my family.

Saffron Nutt (10)
Timmergreens Primary School

Myself

Ewan
Intelligent
Bubbly
Messy
Wishes to discover a new species of dinosaur
Dreams to travel around the world
Who wonders what it would be like as an animal
Or a prehistoric creature
Who fears going underground
Who likes playing the computer
Who hates mushy peas
Who loves chocolate
Who loves animals
Who loves his family, every single one
Who plans to be a palaeontologist
Who plans to go to university
Who plans to name a dinosaur
Ewan.

Ewan Barrack (11)
Timmergreens Primary School

Anger

Anger is red like a dragon breathing boiling hot fire onto me.
It sounds like lightning colliding against the ground.
It looks like a metal display of spikes with blistering hot flames
melting through it.
It smells like my cooker has gone on fire and all I smell is smoke
and flames.
It tastes like burnt barbecue food sizzling in my mouth.
It feels like the veins in my head are going to burst out in an explosion.
It reminds me of horror films that I have watched.

Stephen Brown (10)
Timmergreens Primary School

Myself

Matthew
Who's funny
Who's tall
Who's smart
Who wishes to control time
Who dreams to be rich
Who wonders what it would be like to be famous
Who fears wasps
Who likes spaghetti in a tin
Who loves his family
Who loves Dundee United
Who loves food
Who plans to go to university
Who plans to be an accountant
Who plans to get married,
Matthew.

Matthew Gibson (11)
Timmergreens Primary School

Myself

Dean Hill
Friendly
Spectacular
Funny
Who wishes to be an inventor
Who dreams to go to the moon
Who wonders what it would be like to swim with dolphins
Who fears wasps
Who loves Chinese food
Who hates veg and Brussel sprouts
Who loves his mum
And to lie in his bed
Who plans to go to college
And to learn to drive
Dean Hill.

Dean Hill (10)
Timmergreens Primary School

Myself

Nathan
Funny
Daft
Clever
Wishes to breathe underwater
Dreams of being a billionaire
Who fears of being buried alive
Who likes Lego
Who hates Brussels sprouts
Who loves macaroni
Who loves his family
Who loves chips
Who plans to be a Lego designer
Who plans to be rich
Who plans to be brilliant
Nathan.

Nathan Christie (11)
Timmergreens Primary School

Myself

Katy
Mad
Funny
Kind
Who wishes to go round the world in 80 days
Who dreams of being a lizard
Who wonders if she will get a good life
Who fears the dark very, very much
Who likes going to the park
Who hates shopping lots
Who loves her dog, her brother and her mum
Who plans to work in Disneyland Paris
Who plans to do her best at all times
Who plans to get a pet wizard called Katy.

Katy Waddell (11)
Timmergreens Primary School

Myself

Emma
Friendly
Sociable
Sensible
Wishes to be a lawyer
Who dreams of meeting famous people
Who wonders what it's like to cruise around the world
Who fears of meeting a huge spider
Who likes to go shopping with her friends
Who hates falling out with her friends
Who loves her family
Italian food
Going on holiday
Who plans to go to college and get a good job
Plans to play her trumpet in a concert
Plans to work hard at school, especially maths
Emma.

Emma Finch (11)
Timmergreens Primary School

Love

Love is pink like pretty pink flowers.
It looks like a pretty bunch of long, pink flowers.
It smells like pretty, beautiful, long flowers.
It feels very hot and cosy.
It tastes like melted chocolate.
It sounds very cosy, quiet and happy.
It reminds me of my family.

Shannon Ramsay (10)
Timmergreens Primary School

Myself

Kelly
Friendly
Kind
Happy
Wishes to be a piper
Dreams of flying like a bird
Wonders what it would be like to stand on the moon
Hates spiders
Hates Chinese
Hates Brussels sprouts
Loves Mum
Loves Dad
Wants to have a good life
Who plans to play bagpipes at weddings
Kelly.

Kelly Smeaton (11)
Timmergreens Primary School

Love

Love is red like a love heart
It sounds like a music band playing
It tastes like a flower with big petals on it
It smells like red roses falling down on me
It looks like a big love heart saying, 'I love you'
It feels like happiness is coming to me
It reminds me of happiness all over the world.

Robert Matthew (10)
Timmergreens Primary School

Myself

Rachel
Friendly
Funny
Hyperactive
Wishes to be a paediatrician
Who dreams of flying
Who wonders what it would be like to fly
Who fears dying
Who likes doing ju-jitsu
Who hates ignorant and boastful people
Who loves family
Netball
Table tennis
Who plans to drive
To teach ju-jitsu
To try and pass my highers
And do well in the future
Rachel.

Rachel Falconer (11)
Timmergreens Primary School

Anger

Anger is red like fire burning in my eyes
It sounds like a fire burning in a house
It tastes like a very sour sweet
It smells like smoke burning from a cemetery
It looks like a bad red devil
It feels like jagged spikes, big and huge
It reminds me of tigers roaring noisily.

Declan Johnston (10)
Timmergreens Primary School

Myself

Blair
Nice
Good
Funny
Wishes to drive a car
Dreams of being a multi-millionaire
Who wants to live forever
Who fears big red biting insects in his tent
Who likes scouting
Who hates homework
Who loves fish and chips
Who loves computers
Who loves water
Who plans to get a good house
Who plans to get a good job
Who plans to get a car
Blair.

Blair Wallace (10)
Timmergreens Primary School

Anger

Anger is green like the grass that grows.
It smells like dog's poo.
It tastes like ice cream.
It looks like a volcano about to erupt.
It sounds like a big explosion.
It feels like I am going to pick a fight.
It reminds me of my big brother.

David Penman (10)
Timmergreens Primary School

Myself

Jan
Friendly
Giggly
Kind
Wishes to be a swimmer
Dreams to fly
Who wonders what it would be like to fly
Who fears spiders
Who likes to go shopping with friends
Who hates her brother
Who loves her family
Who loves getting presents
Who loves eating Indian food
Plans to go to college
Plans to try her best in school
Plans to live in America
Jan.

Jan Ramsay (11)
Timmergreens Primary School

Myself

Kane White
Young
Funny
Lazy
Wishes to have everlasting wishes
Dreams of being able to teleport
Who wonders what it would be like to be rich
Fears of dying
Who likes playing football
Who hates teachers and school
Who loves his family
Who loves his pets
Who plans to be a car racer
Kane White.

Kane White (10)
Timmergreens Primary School

Myself

Kerr
Kind
Funny
Organised
Who wishes to be an archaeologist
Dreams to be able to breathe underwater
Who wonders what it would be like to travel to the other galaxies
Who fears being in a small underground area
Who likes playing his accordion
Who hates people being nasty to him
Who loves eating chocolates
Who loves playing with his friends and pets
Who loves his family
Who plans to drive a car
Who plans to be an archaeologist
Who plans to go to Australia
Kerr.

Kerr Barrack (11)
Timmergreens Primary School

Myself

James
Caring
Careful
Noisy
Wishes to get a Porsche
Dreams of being a multi-millionaire
Who wonders what it's like to be my dad
Fears nothing
Hates maths
Loves his family
Who plans to drive
James.

James Twaddle (11)
Timmergreens Primary School

Myself

Aaron
Crazy
Lazy
Funny
Wishes to be a motocross driver
Dreams of being Spider-Man
Who wonders what it is like to be Spider-Man
Who fears of dying
Who likes driving motorbikes
Who hates school
Who loves food
Football
Motorbikes
Who plans to drive a car
And be a footballer
Aaron.

Aaron Robb (10)
Timmergreens Primary School

Anger

Anger is black like a dark tunnel
It sounds like hammers in my head non-stop
It tastes like a Bombay Bad Boy sizzling on my tongue
It smells like a raging fire spreading all over
It feels like scraping rock against metal
It reminds me of my brother.

Jack McAllan (9)
Timmergreens Primary School

Myself

Ellis
Mad
Silly
Noisy
Wishes to live in Paris
Dreams of going to the future
Who wonders what it would be like to be a fish
Who fears big creepy crawly spiders
Who likes to play netball and dance
Who hates boys
Who loves her family
Who loves pasta
Who also loves to dance
Who plans to learn to drive
Who plans to go to college
Who plans to be a PE teacher
Ellis.

Ellis Munro (10)
Timmergreens Primary School

Love

Love is red like love hearts
It sounds like soft singing
It tastes like hot chocolate with marshmallows
It smells like lovely perfume
It looks like love hearts shining everywhere
It feels like I'm so cosy and so happy, loved over and over again.

Kayleigh Crumlish (10)
Timmergreens Primary School